Letters from India

Carolyn Potts Hayward

To order additional copies of this book, contact:
Xlibris Corporation
1-888-795-4274
www.Xlibris.com
Orders@Xlibris.com
48657

CONTENTS

A Fool Lies Here

Now it is not good for the Christian's health to hustle the Aryan brown, For the Christian riles, and the Aryan smiles and he weareth the Christian down; At the end of the fight is a tombstone white with the name of the last deceased, And the epitaph drear: "A fool lies here who tried to hustle the East."

—Rudyard Kipling

Rudyard Kipling knew India well, and his words sum up what my mother would later find out to be the reality of the many years she lived in India.

Virginia, Ginny, Gia, or Muggie
Beautiful by any name

PREFACE

Nashua, New Hampshire, July 31, 2003:

Why does someone write a book? I am sure there are many reason. Some are a desire to impart a thought. Sometimes it is to inform you of another views, and sometimes it is just a story that comes from the heart.

Just about six weeks ago, our family gathered on the beautiful island of Nantucket, Massachusetts, to celebrate my mother's ninetieth birthday. Today—her actual birthday—she is far away in Texas, celebrating with her friends from Mexico, where she lived for twenty-two years.

My daughter Megan and I were discussing "Gea's" incredible life, marveling at how a blind date on October 13, 1936, led to a lifetime of travel and adventure. Few people ever have a life so full, lived in places all over the world; even fewer find a love like that of Ginny and Ned's, which endured for fifty-six years until my father's death in 1992.

Fortunately for me, when Ginny and Ned first traveled halfway around the world to begin their new life together in India, she wrote daily letters to her family, relating their experiences, sometimes fascinating and often frustrating. Here, all these years later, we can read about the details of their early life, from 1936 to 1943. Those letters, plus the photo essay she and my father kept of their travels and all the stories she told me through the years—motivated me to want to share her story. Typically self-effacing, Ginny thinks the idea is silly ("Who would want to read about *me*?"), but undeterred, I started gathering material and writing notes.

September 25, 2004:

Sadly, Ginny died before she was able to read her book. I am so grateful that before she died, I recorded interviews with her. Her recollections, along with her letters, made the book possible.

She passed away at the age of ninety-one, and she did it in style as only Ginny could. She had gone to the theater with friends, and afterward they were enjoying dinner at a Mexican restaurant. She ordered a gin martini; she took a couple of sips, said, "I have a pain in my chest," set her head on the table, and was gone. Her friends and family miss her enormously; she was an extraordinary woman who touched the hearts of so many.

February 2009:

As the book nears completion, I have chosen to tell the story from Ginny's point of view. This has entailed some imagining of thoughts and words on my part, but the facts are accurate, and I have used my memories of her stories and exact words from her own letters whenever possible. I hope the reader will get to know my extraordinary mother through this attempt of mine to bring her tale the acknowledgment it deserves.

Mom this book is a testament to your courage and strength.

Carolyn "Cali" Hayward

INTRODUCTION

Minneapolis, Minnesota:

I was born on a hot July day in 1913 to Hama and John Ray and given the name Virginia Thompson Ray. Our family lived in Minneapolis until 1923, after the birth of my brother, John Henry II, who was named for my father and called Jack. My father, an aspiring young lawyer with a degree from Harvard, worked for Western Electric—a new company at the time, soon to become a giant in the industry and later to be known as AT&T. When Father was hired to work in the legal division in the corporate offices in New York City, he moved our family to Staten Island, New York, where my brother Gordon was born in 1928.

The Ray Family in 1936: Virginia, John, Gordon, and Jack Hama.

Thanks to Father's job as a corporate attorney, our family was fortunate
to escape the economic hardships suffered by many people during the Great
Depression, from 1929 to 1933. We lived quite comfortably on Staten
Island; Jack, Gordon, and I attended private schools, and I enjoyed spending
time with friends and playing golf at the Richmond Hills Country Club
on Dongan Hills.

I never imagined when I graduated from high school at eighteen how
dramatically my life would change by the time I turned twenty-three—all
because I dared to say yes to an impetuous proposal.

A reversal of roles. Mr. Evens of Hyde Park, MA, is the gentleman
in a lady's attire. "What a good-looking couple we made."

CHAPTER ONE

A Clash of Wills

1931:

I had just graduated from Miss Choate School for Girls in Boston. The years there were filled with many memories, especially the school plays where, because of my height, I always played the male role.

Virginia, the gladiator in the play *Alexander*

I had not been the best student, and the thought of more school was the farthest thing from my mind. I was in no hurry to make any big decisions about my future. I casually perused the Help Wanted ads in the newspaper. Jobs for Men listed a variety of options while Jobs for Women were limited to nursing, teaching, secretarial work, or domestic positions.

Women had just won the right to vote a little more than a decade ago, and the women's liberation movement was another forty years in the future. At the time, men held most of the positions of power, and young women were simply expected to find a good husband, stay home, and raise a family.

Miss Choate School 1931 graduation photo

I had made it through high school all right, but I wasn't giving college a second thought. At eighteen, I wasn't sure about too much, but I was certain of one thing: I was done with school.

Father had other ideas though. He was determined that no child of his, male or female, was going to stay home and waste time. He was a man with a very strong sense of duty and pride. "Ginny, you only get out of life what you put into it," he admonished me. "You don't make a mark by just standing by." If college didn't appeal to me, he said, then maybe I should try secretarial school.

Without much enthusiasm, I enrolled in a two-year secretarial program at Katherine Gibbs School in New York City. Father made it clear that he hoped the experience would encourage me to go on to college.

After a year at Katherine Gibbs, however, I decided I had had enough of school—it was too much like work, right down to having to look the part by wearing a dress, heels, hat, and white gloves to class every day.

All dressed up for school

I came home and announced to Father that I was quitting secretarial school. As you can imagine, he wasn't at all happy to hear this news. He told me I couldn't abandon a job until it was finished, no matter how distasteful it was. He insisted that I go back to school and finish what I had started. I refused—I felt pretty strongly myself. (I wonder where I acquired my stubborn streak.)

But for Father, quitting simply was not an option. He gave me more time to reflect on my decision, certain that I would come around to seeing things his way. Well, I did give it some thought all that night, and the next day, I decided my first choice was best: I would quit school.

I wasn't prepared for the ultimatum Father handed down in response: return to school or no more telephone!

My best friend Dot and I, taken in a photo machine at Coney Island

I was back in school the next day. The telephone was my only means of communicating with my friends, especially my best friend, Dot Garrett. I was convinced at the time that life simply wasn't worth living without a phone. Little did I know that I would later spend years without one.

KATHERINE GIBBS SCHOOL
New York

December 3, 1934

To Whom It May Concern:

Miss Virginia Ray attended our school during the years 1931-33, taking a Two—Year Course, the first is collegiate and the second technical in nature. Combined, the course gave Miss Ray a good informational background and a careful training in secretarial requirements. She did good work and received a Two-Year certificate from the school upon completion of the course.
We found Miss Ray to be alert, intelligent, and industrious. Her background, her personality, and her contact ability should appeal to those who value those qualities.

Very sincerely yours,

Adelaide B Hawkins
Technical Director

I may have been a reluctant student, but I developed excellent secretarial skills at Katherine Gibbs School. Degree in hand, I landed my first job at Columbia Presbyterian Hospital in New York City, working in the social services department with three other women. Each day, it would take me an hour and a half to travel one way to work: first the car ride to the station, then the train to the ferry, the ferry to the city, then the subway to Bowling Green Station, and finally on foot to the hospital; I took my first paycheck to George Jensens to buy Mother a silver pin.

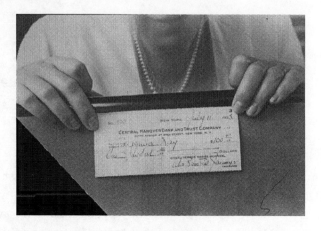

My first paycheck

I spent a year working at Columbia Presbyterian Hospital before leaving the job to drive my grandmother Gracie to Los Angeles. Gracie had rented an apartment across the street from movie star Mae West.

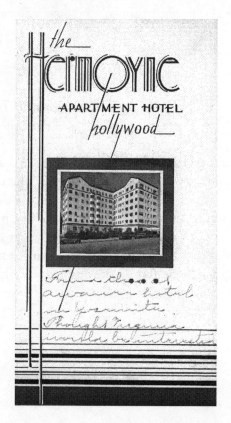

This was my first time traveling out of the Northeast, so I took some time to explore the sights in Los Angeles. But after a few months, I was anxious to get back home. I missed my family and was lonely for my friends.

Once back in New York, I found a job with Laying-In Hospital, a branch of New York Cornell. I was working for the head of the first pediatric psychiatry department in the country and was happy with the work when my old boss from Columbia Presbyterian, Virginia Kinzel, offered me a job as a social worker in their social services department.

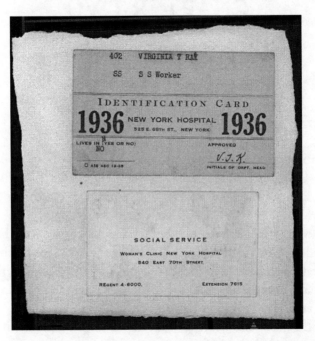

Even though I didn't have a degree in social work, Virginia felt I would do an outstanding job. I accepted the social work position at Columbia Presbyterian, and Virginia and I quickly became close friends. At the time, her husband, Bob, was working for a large company, Union Carbide, and did a lot of traveling. Whenever he was away, I would stay at Virginia's apartment in the city. It was so nice not to have the long commute back and forth to Staten Island. It led me to dreaming about getting a place of my own in the city, maybe even marrying a doctor and settling down.

My dream of marrying a doctor wasn't that far-fetched. I had been dating Dr. Goodman, an intern at the hospital, for nearly two years, and while the romance was going slowly—he wanted to finish his internship before making any plans for the future—I thought he just might be "the one."

CHAPTER TWO

Thirteen is a Lucky Number

Fall 1936:

Virginia's husband, Bob, had told her that one of his colleagues from Union Carbide, a Canadian named James Edward "Ned" Potts, had just moved to the city; and she thought the four of us should go out for a night on the town.

I hesitated at first. "I'm dating Dr. Goodman," I protested, "I don't think it's a good idea." But Virginia seemed sure of this match. She persisted, telling me that Ned was six-feet-five-inches tall and very handsome, with blue eyes and curly dark brown hair. "He's quite the lady's man," she said with a grin. "What do you have to lose by agreeing to just one date?"

Well, all I needed to hear was that he was six-feet-five-inches tall, and my objections faded. At six feet tall myself, I'd found it hard to meet men who were taller than me. Frankly, I was tired of being hunched over on the dance floor all the time. Most of the men I had gone out with were shorter than I was, and when we danced, their heads were at my breasts. It would be great to actually have a man I could look in the eyes. On October 13, we all agreed to meet after work at a place in the city called the Monkey Bar.

The young Canadian

Originally from Stirling, a very small town in Ontario, Canada, Ned, had been living at the Lexington Hotel since moving to the city. He had heard a lot about me from Virginia and Bob and was anxiously awaiting our date as much as I was.

Bob and Virginia Kinzel

I wasn't disappointed when I met him—he was everything Virginia described and more. The four of us talked and laughed until late into the evening. I was intrigued by this tall, outgoing Canadian with beautiful blue eyes. I learned that he was an only child and that his father, Jim, who had been a doctor in Stirling, had passed away during his first year of college, leaving Ned to pay his way through university by digging ditches and building roads.

He had earned an electrical engineering degree from McGill University in Montreal; and his best friend and college roommate, Buster, had married Ned's longtime friend, Peggy. Peggy and her mother had lived with Ned's family for a while, and Ned's mother, Minn, had hoped she would become her daughter-in-law. However, when Peggy visited Ned at college, she fell in love with his roommate, Buster; and they were married shortly after graduation.

Ned and I had an instant attraction to each other. We just couldn't seem to take our eyes off each other all night. He confided to Bob the next day that he thought I was one of the most stunning and beautiful women he'd ever met. That's a compliment any woman would love to hear! At the end of our evening at the Monkey Bar, Ned and I shared a cab ride.

I was headed to Margaret Sutter's apartment in the city, and he was headed back to his room at the Lexington Hotel. Margaret was a close family friend who invited me to stay at her place whenever I didn't want to make the long commute home or if Virginia's extra bed wasn't available.

During the cab ride, Ned took my hand in his and said, "I had a swell time tonight, Ginny. Will you go out with me again?" This time there was no hesitation on my part. "Yes, that would be wonderful," I said, my heart pounding. We agreed to meet on Saturday for lunch at Schrafft's. When Virginia caught wind of our plans, she said Schrafft's was far too ordinary and suggested we try a more intimate, upscale place called Tony Trauvelles. I called Ned the next day to tell him about the change in restaurants.

It was past noon when I called, but to my surprise, he answered the phone in a groggy voice. He said he'd been out with a date the previous night and was "just surfacing." I thought, "Ladies' man, indeed!" and had to admit I was a little jealous. It wasn't until later that I learned that nearly everyone he knew in New York had been setting him up on blind dates. The poor man was exhausted.

"Ladies' man, indeed."

On our second date, we had lunch at Tony Trauvelles, and then we went shopping to buy Ned a new hat. It seems he had left his at his date's house the night before, and no well-dressed man of the time went out without a fedora. (Secretly, I was happy he wasn't planning to go back to his date's house to retrieve his hat!) I watched as Ned tried on hats and chatted amiably with the sales staff. It seemed to me that this smooth-talking Canadian was able to get along well with everyone he met.

From there we headed to Radio City Music Hall to see the world famous dancers the Rockettes, followed by a movie. It's a good thing the Rockettes were impressive because the movie wasn't particularly a man's show. We saw *Little Women*—or I should say I saw it; Ned slept all the way through it. I half thought it would be fun to sneak into the row behind him and watch him wake up and wonder where I'd gone. But then I decided he might not see the humor in my little prank.

After the movie, we were both too tired for another night on the town, yet we weren't quite ready to part company. So Ned decided to take the ferry with me to Staten Island. I could hardly believe how close we felt after just two dates. It was a long good-bye at the dock in Staten Island before Ned took the next boat back to the city. I didn't know where our relationship was headed, but I had already decided one thing: my relationship with Dr. Goodman was over. The man I once thought about settling down with just didn't compare to the tall, handsome, and debonair James "Ned" Potts.

Tall, handsome, and debonair, no question!

October 1936:

Ned made a trip back to Montreal to attend his five-year McGill reunion. He had tried to coax me to come along so he could introduce me to his college buddies, but after just two dates, I felt that our relationship was too new to take a long trip together. I did agree to meet him at the train station when he returned.

Ned—W. Hulbig—Buster

So there I stood at Grand Central Station, waiting for Ned. Except when the train pulled into the station, Ned wasn't on it. I started to stew. Was he disappointed with me for not going with him? Was he not interested in me after all? I went home, angry and upset, thinking maybe this guy wasn't worth it after all.

The next day, he called me at work to apologize profusely. Turned out he had an opportunity to ride home from Montreal with some friends, and he had no way to reach me to let me know. I can't say for sure who was happier—me or Ned—when we agreed to pick up our relationship where we'd left off a week ago.

On October 27, 1936 (just fourteen days after we'd first met), Ned and I agreed to meet at Bill's Gay Nineties, a New York City landmark in the theater district that is frequented by celebrities. We were greeted by a doorman, dressed in white pants, a black vest, and a straw hat. With his large handlebar mustache, he looked like he should be singing in a barbershop quartet. It was like stepping back in time to the days when the place was one of the first speakeasies in New York.

Like all guests at Bill's Gay Nineties, we were each given a handlebar mustache to wear when we walked in. The walls on the main floor are covered with photos of Ziegfeld Girls from the 1880s and autographed pictures of Buffalo Bill and Al Jolson, just to name a few celebrities from all walks of life, a history of time since it was established in the early twenties. More often than not, you can spot someone famous among the guests. The piano bar where we sat had a sporting theme—photos of jockeys and boxers fill the walls—and the piano player encouraged everyone to sing along. It took no time at all for Ned and I to feel comfortable there. Ned had played the cornet and had been the bandleader at McGill University. He obviously had music in his blood and also loved to sing, a passion that I soon discovered was fueled even further after he'd had a few drinks.

Ned and I talked about our families, our schooling, and our jobs. I told him that my thirteen-year-old brother, Jack, hoped to become a doctor someday, and Gordon, just eight, was in second grade. Ned told me that after graduating from McGill, he couldn't find a job, so he continued to dig ditches and build roads. One cold day, he wore his McGill sweater to work, his supervisor, Mr. George Rainer, asked Ned if he had gone to McGill and had a college degree. Ned told him yes. He had a degree in electrical engineering, then Mr. Rainer asked him why on earth was he still digging ditches.

"Easy. I can't find a job," Ned replied.

Mr. Rainer told Ned he had a friend who could probably get him a job as a salesman for the Union Carbide Company. Ned's job in Canada as a salesman with exceptional skills landed him in New York City, where he was being groomed for a sales position overseas. Union Carbide Company at the time was looking to expand the sale of its flashlights and other battery products into non-industrialized areas like India, Africa, Singapore, and the Far East. In 1936, flashlights would bring light to people in the small villages still living without electricity.

Years later, when Ned and I were on "home leave," we would visit Mr. Rainer so Ned could thank him for his help. I remember how shocked Mr. Rainer was by the visit. "In all my years of helping SOBs, you're the only SOB who ever came back to thank me," he said.

Ned and I talked and drank well into the evening at Bill's Gay Nineties, both of us getting a little giddy. At one point, the photo gal came over to snap our picture. As Ned and I moved closer for the shot, a gentleman sitting next to us remarked what a stunning couple we were and asked Ned if that beautiful woman was his wife. "Not yet," Ned said with a twinkle in his eye.

No one was more stunned than I was when a short time later Ned actually popped the question, "Ginny, will you marry me?"

I thought for only half a second before replying, "Yes, of course!" My heart was racing, and I felt like the luckiest girl in the city. I was smiling so hard I thought I would stay that way forever. Oh my! What a moment it was.

After the initial shock and the blood had returned to my head, we decided to elope. Neither one of us had any idea what to do or where to go to make it happen. Did we need a marriage license and a blood test? We had so many questions, and at 1:00 a.m., after an evening of drinking, we decided Virginia would have all the answers. After all, she was married, and she should know what needed to be done. We went to the phone booth, and I sat on Ned's lap. We were both holding the phone to our ears, waiting for her words of wisdom. The call startled her from a sound sleep, and excitedly, both of us at the same time told her our news. Virginia was obviously thinking more clearly than we were, and she may had been half asleep, but she was sober and not in a giddy state of happiness. "Are you sure you're not being too hasty?" She took a deep breath and added, "You only just had your third date. Why don't you go home and sleep on it?"

Reluctantly, Ned and I agreed. We were caught up in the excitement and probably should give it some time to sink in. We called it a night and caught a cab to Margaret's apartment where we had a long kiss good night, then Ned went back to the Lexington Hotel.

I was so excited when I told Margaret about our plans that night; she tried to talk some sense into me. After all, she was one of Mother's dearest friends, and she must have felt she needed to do something to nip this foolish plan in the bud. "Ginny, you've had too much to drink. Why don't you just go to bed, and we'll have a talk in the morning."

The next day, when clearer heads prevailed, Ned and I decided maybe we shouldn't elope just yet. After all, he was living in a hotel, and I was still living at home with my parents. Gee, Mother and Father hadn't even met Ned yet, and they surely wouldn't be too happy about our plans.

There was no doubt in my mind I loved Ned, and he loved me, but we thought maybe we had been a little too hasty. So we devised a plan: we would meet at Schrafft's for lunch the next day. It would give us a little time to think and to figure out if our judgment had been clouded by too much alcohol the night before. Or if it was really love. The plan was if one of us had second thoughts and decided not to get married, he or she would not show up for lunch. We both agreed our plan would allow us to back out gracefully, if necessary, without meeting face-to-face.

CHAPTER THREE

Do We Say "I Do"?

I was a little late getting to Schrafft's and was disappointed to see that Ned was nowhere in sight. What had happened? Had he grown tired of waiting for me, or had he thought that my late "no show" was a sign that I wanted to back out? Maybe he regretted proposing to me after all? I sat at Schrafft's, disappointed and overwhelmed about what to do next.

Should I give up and go back to work or order lunch and hope he might show up late after all? My head was spinning, and tears were burning my eyes when I spotted Ned coming toward me. My heart began to race, and my stomach fluttered nervously. As soon as our eyes met, I knew that he was just as happy to see me as I was to see him! The waitress came over and asked Ned what he would like for lunch. He said, "I will have a peanut butter and bacon sandwich." She asked if he would like some spread on the bread, and he said, "Thousand Island, thanks." It was obvious he wasn't even paying attention to what the waitress said.

He apologized for being so late, explaining that he'd been called back to the office at the last minute and had no way to reach me to let me know.

"I was so afraid you would think I had changed my mind and would leave," Ned said breathlessly, taking me in his arms. We agreed that "fate" meant for us to be together. We decided during lunch to try and keep our engagement a secret and to announce it to our families and friends at Christmastime. That was going to be hard, seeing we had already spilled the beans to Margaret and Virginia.

But fate had other plans. Just a few days later, Ned learned that he was about to be assigned to a sales position in India. He would be leaving in just a few short weeks. To make things worse, Union Carbide only sent single men overseas. His supervisors explained to him that the salary was for only one person and that life in India would be very difficult; he would need to make do with few of the comforts of home. It just wasn't a suitable environment for a woman.

Ned faced a dilemma. He loved me and was intent on getting married. He also wanted to accept the company's offer to work overseas. Quickly, he decided he wasn't going anywhere without me. I was happy he felt so strongly and that it was true love not just a passing fancy.

When his supervisor, Alex MacKenzie, heard of Ned's situation, he told a colleague to "fire the bastard." He had no patience for this mess and had no time for employees who were unwilling to conform to company rules.

Ned decided to take matters into his own hands and called the company president, Mr. Vander Poel, who blew his top. He wasn't too happy to be disturbed at home on a Sunday. "Can't this wait until Monday?" he asked.

Once he heard about Ned's situation, however, Mr. Vander Poel decided he didn't want to lose this promising young employee who seemed perfect for the job. He decided he would have to meet me personally to assess my suitability to go to India with Ned. Mr. Vander Poel told Ned that his bride-to-be would have to be an asset to the company and a woman capable of withstanding the hardships of living in India, or Ned would have to choose between getting married or staying with Union Carbide.

I had a meeting with the president. I was nervous but full of confidence that I could win him over and make him not regret the decision to let me go. Luckily, I charmed and impressed Mr. Vander Poel, and he gave us his approval for me to go to India. Now I had the hardest job of all. I just had to get my parents' blessing to marry Ned and move eight thousand miles away from home. It wasn't going to be easy.

Mother tried to tell me I was making a big mistake. "You just met the man. You can't possibly be sure you love him," she said. She told me that if our love was real, it would survive a long separation. Father weighed in with his opinion as well, telling me that I was being hasty and impulsive and should give this some serious thought. Father chose his words very carefully and was always sure he had said what he needed to say in a manner that was concise.

But my mind was made up. My love for Ned and his love for me was very powerful. No one, not even my family, could talk me out of marrying him and following him to a strange country halfway around the world. Ned's first letter to me made me realize that he was the man I wanted to spend the rest of my life with.

9pm

My darling mug

Or should I say just plain mug, anyway darling I love you and now that I have
been gone for an hour it's getting bad. Gee I still can't believe how lucky I am.
I hope you don't get tired of hearing the same three words over and over again,
because I am afraid you're going to hear them for a long time my sweet.
I wish your mother could keep the old chin up. It's tough to lose you but it would
be so much easier for her if she could. I feel so badly after all darling It's not an
entire loss cause you will be back in three years, and the mail still functions
and I'll do my damnedest to make you happy.
Here is the old sentimental side coming out that's bad.
Darling I can't say anything except that I love you over and over again-and
like the quotation in the Delhi Temple "If time is a paradise in love, then please
don't waken me."
I have never never felt like this before now and how I love it. I have left a call
for 6:30—so pleasant dreams my sweet and all my love to the sweetest girl in
the whole wide world. Try and keep your mother smiling, and give my best to
everyone. I wish I could see you again your Mug,
Again all my love darling, Ned

(Mug was short for Muggie, which was Ned's pet name for me. It all
started after we had our passport photos taken.)

Our engagement photo 1936

CHAPTER FOUR

Setting Sail

New York, New York:

We had only a few weeks to plan our wedding and to get ready for our new life in India. One challenge was finding clothes—this was in the days before specialty shops sold cruise wear year-round. It was cold in New York in November and would be chilly as we set sail from the harbor in New York on our first leg to London. Yet we knew that once we reached India, it would be very hot. I also had the added challenge of my height. I was six feet tall at a time when the average woman was five feet four inches. It was rare for me to buy dressy clothes off the rack; everything had to be fitted or custom-made. Besides, I had no idea what the well-dressed women of India was wearing in 1936.

Fortunately, Mother and I received help from Mrs. Dodge, the wife of Mr. Dodge from Dodge and Seymour, the company that was representing Union Carbide in India. Dodge and Seymour was an agency that tested overseas markets for companies like Union Carbide. With foreign trade still a new practice—their groundwork determined if it made financial sense to set up and staff sales offices. Mrs. Dodge had lived in India for many years and was helpful in advising me about what to bring—including summer weight slacks, skirts, blouses, and day frocks. Without her advice, it would be hard to know what was needed in a place so different from New York.

Mr. and Mrs. John Henry Ray
have the honour of
announcing the marriage of their daughter
Virginia Thompson
to
Mr. James Edward Potts
Wednesday, the twenty-fifth of November
One thousand, nine hundred and thirty-six
New York

Mr. and Mrs. James Edward Potts

c/o Dodge and Seymour
Tower House
Chowringhee Square
Calcutta, India

Wednesday, November 25, 1936, Our Wedding Day:

Ned and I had decided to get married in New York City at the Little Church Around the Corner. It was going to be a small affair, with only family and close friends in attendance—Mother, Father, my brothers, Jack and Gordon, Ned's mother, Minn, my best friend, Dot Garrett, and Virginia and bob Kinzel.

The ceremony would take place at nine in the morning at the church, and then we would go to the ship for a small reception on board before setting sail at noon the same day.

With our wedding only a few hours away, a series of small mishaps started to unfold. First, Father forgot to fill his car with gas the night before, so he had to stop on the way to the city, and we missed the ferry from Staten Island to New York.

The Church of the Transfiguration. Better known as The Little Church Around the Corner an Episcopal church located at One East Twenty-ninthe Street between Fifth Avenue and Madison Avenue, New York, New York.

We had to wait for the next ferry, making us a little late for the church. Turned out Ned was late too. He flagged down a cab at Forty-second Street and asked the cabbie to hurry and "get him to the church on time." Well, with the cab headed in the wrong direction, the cabbie decided to pull a U-turn. Just their luck, a policeman saw the illegal turn and blew his whistle, motioning the cab to the curb. Ned and the cabbie had to wait while the officer wrote out a traffic ticket.

Finally, everyone arrived at the church, and the ceremony began, with the Reverend Randolph Ray (no relation to us) performing the service. Ned and I chose to keep things simple and did not have any wedding attendants. I wore a navy blue crepe street dress trimmed in fuchsia and a matching felt hat. I didn't carry a handheld bouquet, which would have been traditional. Instead, I wore a corsage of orchids and lilies. The only thing traditional about our wedding was the vows.

As soon as the church service was over, we all made a mad dash for the ship, scheduled to leave port at noon. Well, our luck that day continued, except this time it turned out to be good luck. The ship was late getting into port due to a storm at sea and was now scheduled to set sail at 3:00 p.m. Father decided to take advantage of the extra time to take everyone to lunch at Longchamps Restaurant.

It was a bittersweet wedding celebration. Though we had just met a few short weeks ago, Ned and I were deeply in love and so happy to be starting our lives as "Mr. and Mrs. James Edward Potts." We were excited about the adventure awaiting us, but at the same time, we were sad to be leaving our friends and family.

Mr. and Mrs. James Potts on board the *Berengaria,* Wednesday before sailing to Europe en route to India where they will reside. Mrs. Potts is the former Miss. Virginia Thompson Ray of Dongon Hills. Staten Island, New York

Our impromptu reception at Longchamps was such fun and seemed like the best wedding present of all. We were toasted many times, wished "Godspeed for a happy and wonderful life" and "Good fortune."

Just before we were getting ready to leave the restaurant, I excused myself to visit the ladies' room. Mother was right behind me and surprised me by asking everyone to leave so she could talk to me. When I turned to face her, there were tears in her eyes.

"Ginny, I don't think you should be going to India. You're making a huge mistake," she said, sobbing quietly. "Please tell Ned that you've changed your mind. If he loves you, he'll understand. He really will," she went on, her distress rising.

I was fighting back tears as I put my arms around her and I told Mother everything was going to be fine. I would be with the man I loved, and we were about to begin the adventure of a lifetime.

Mother was not convinced. "If things don't work out," she said, "I want you to send me a cable with the message 'House in Flames,' and Father and I will send you the money for boat fare home."

It was a nice offer. But in my heart, I had never been surer of anything in my whole life. Even though Ned and I didn't know each other well, I felt certain the love we shared was strong enough to see us through the challenges of living so far from home in a strange, new country.

My resolve about leaving my family and friends almost faded, however, as we boarded the RMS *Berengaria* headed for Southampton, England, amid streamers, blowing horns, and many tears. Ned and I were both fighting back tears ourselves as we waved good-bye to Mother, Father, Minn, Jack, Gordon, and Dot. Suddenly, I was overwhelmed with sadness as I realized I would not see my family for three years. On board the ship, we would be surrounded by the ocean and unfamiliar faces for many weeks. Who knew what awaited us in India? Would our whirlwind romance withstand the challenges ahead?

"Last call," Virginia and Bob aboard ship with Ned and Ginny

CHAPTER FIVE

No Turning Back Now

Somewhere in the Atlantic Ocean:

Our honeymoon began below ship, in a small cabin filled with baskets of food, fruit, and flowers. We shared a bottle of champagne and read cables from many well-wishers. My first letter home gave a short glimpse into the first couple of days of our journey.

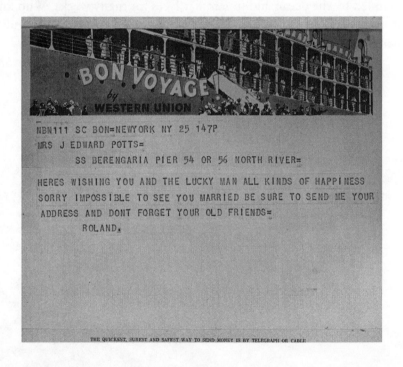

BON VOYAGE by WESTERN UNION

NBN111 SC BON=NEWYORK NY 25 147P

MRS J EDWARD POTTS=

  SS BERENGARIA PIER 54 OR 56 NORTH RIVER=

HERES WISHING YOU AND THE LUCKY MAN ALL KINDS OF HAPPINESS

SORRY IMPOSSIBLE TO SEE YOU MARRIED BE SURE TO SEND ME YOUR

ADDRESS AND DONT FORGET YOUR OLD FRIENDS=

  ROLAND.

THE QUICKEST, SUREST AND SAFEST WAY TO SEND MONEY IS BY TELEGRAPH OR CABLE

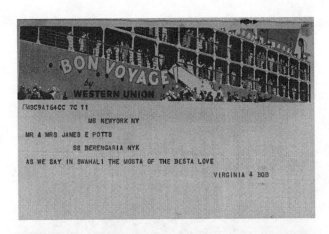

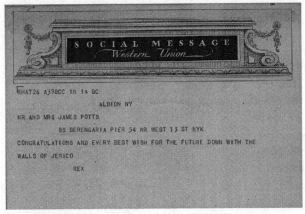

Passport photo or mug shots?

Cunard White Star   Berengaria

Four weeks at sea
On board the White Star ship *Berengaria*

Dearest All,
It was hard to say good-bye at Longchamps because there were so
many things I wanted to say but couldn't. Please know how much
I love and miss you. I wish you could see our poor steward trying
to get rid of all the rice and confetti. Never have I seen so much. It
was in the bed, in the bathtub, in every glass and cupboard, not to
mention our pockets and I'm still finding it in things in our trunk.
We took some pictures of the cabin and if they come out I'll show
them to you when you come to India, which I hope will be soon. The
sea has been quite calm all the way with just a little steady roll.
Neither one of us has even felt like "tossing our cookies." Tonight
the steward has asked us to his cabin (for drinks) but I can't have
anything because I got my typhoid shot today. Feel fine though.

All the love in the world,
Virginia

P.S. Almost forgot, Mother, I had Dover sole the first night out, in
honor of you, along with the champagne Mrs. McLeod had sent us.
Both were swell; In fact I've had sole several times since.

The *Berengaria*'s passenger list was an interesting mix of people. Some were going home to jobs and families while others were going around the world to leisurely explore foreign lands. Our first night onboard, we were invited to a cocktail party in the purser's cabin, where everyone toasted us and wished us a life of happiness and good fortune. Our first week onboard the ship was chilly.

Ginny all bundled up on deck. *Burr.*

We spent the time meeting new friends, sitting on deck all bundled up to keep warm, and watching an occasional movie. We saw Jack Holt, Fay Wray, and Ralph Graves in *Dirigible*, which was very interesting but a bit dry. We also saw *Call of the Prairie*, which starred William Boyd and Jimmy Ellison. It was a great Western filled with lots of shooting and trick riding, a real action-packed saga where Hopalong Cassidy saves the day. Ned and I enjoyed it very much.

Southampton, England:

We docked in Southampton and took a train to London, where we stayed at the Savoy Hotel.

The Savoy Hotel in London

The attraction Ned most wanted to see in London was the changing of the guard at Buckingham Palace. It was a magnificent sight! We also spent three hours in Westminster Abbey, where our excellent guide knew every corner and its complete history. I felt awed by the sense of age and tradition. While we were there, they were installing lights and amplifiers for the upcoming coronation of King Edward VIII.

SS *Rawalpindi*

Somewhere in the Mediterranean Sea:

We left Southampton on December 4 aboard the SS *Rawalpindi*, a Peninsular and Oriental (P&O) Navigation Company ship. I posted a letter home shortly after we left port:

Dearest All:

Both of us are crazy about London and want to spend at least a week there on our way back. We didn't have half enough time.

The P & O line is certainly a come down after the Berengaria. Our room of course is much smaller but is an outside cabin. The bath is directly across the hall so it makes it convenient. All over there are signs warning you of the dishonesty of people. It's funny.

They have a bugler who blows a bugle for everything. About as bad as boarding school. The crowd here is very much older than we are but there seem to be many interesting faces. I wish you could see the Hindu waiters when they go ashore as stevedores. Very bright blue stitched tunics over their pants and brilliant red and striped turbans on their heads. The boat is small and rocked like a tub last night but so far both of us have eaten lots of the rotten food on board and loved every minute.

Much love to you all and by the time you get this it will be near Christmas so please know how much we shall be missing you, loving you and sending you all the very best.

Virginia

P.S. Wish you could see me trying to use a dial telephone over here. They certainly are different . . . did I ever feel dumb. I finally hailed a man who was passing and asked him to do it for me. What a life.

On board the *Rawalpindi*, we were assigned to dine at the surgeon's table, where we found a mix of international travelers. Ned was dismayed to discover that the ship bore of a gentleman from Gibraltar; a know-it-all of about forty years old was at our table. Fortunately, he would be getting off soon, so we wouldn't have to listen to his nattering for long.

At the other end of our table were two Scottish lasses and their father, en route to Bombay on holiday. They were so polite and quiet that they had nothing interesting to add to the conversation. Sitting directly across from them was the young and attractive Mrs. George, who was going to meet her husband in Singapore. All the men at our table were intrigued by her.

Next was Miss Bonny, an Englishwoman headed to Bombay, who never said much, and finally there was a doctor going to Penang. He told us he'd been living in the Far East for years and loved it so much he wouldn't think of living anywhere else.

It wasn't until two days later when two chaps from Scotland joined our table that the real fun began. Colin Inglis was a young architect headed to Singapore. He was very nice and always managed to get everyone laughing. The other chap, Mr. MacPherson or Mac, was going to Shanghai. Mac's father was the chairman of the P&O Line. We never missed an opportunity to tease him about the service, all in good fun, of course.

Gibraltar, Spain:

After a brief one-hour stop in Tangier, followed by two more hours at sea, we were finally able to go ashore in Gibraltar. It felt good just to stand on solid ground. Ned hired a *ghari*, and we took a romantic moonlit ride to the Rock Hotel and then back to town.

Marseilles, France:

We spent several days in Marseilles, wandering the streets with our new friends, Colin and Mac. Fortunately for us, Colin spoke French and did most of the talking.

We ate lunch at small sidewalk cafes, drank wine, and enjoyed the sights. Marseilles had colorful outdoor markets filled with fruits and trinkets. Ned bought me a silver charm from an elderly woman vendor and had it engraved "October 13," the date we met. We even took in a French movie.

In a letter home to my folks, Ned described some of the sights:

Marseilles:

One pleasant sight was in a fish stall where a young girl clerk grabbed up a live octopus and slapped it on the counter to make it wriggle—all the while shouting to the passersby. In fact the people in all the stalls seemed to shout and it was a most interesting experience. We also saw our first public wash house—three women washing their clothes in the public fountain. They weren't bothered at all when we took pictures.

The streets were not laid out in any way at all (not blocks) and as we looked up, we could see the washing hanging on lines across the street.

Nearly all of the butcher shops had immense carcasses (horses) hung on nails outside in the street, as well as immense hunks of bloody red liver dripping on the sidewalk. Sausages were sold in rolls, so much a foot and the roll wound around a gigantic cone. On one little square, we heard music and seeing a crowd, [we] went over. A young boy and girl were playing accordions and an older woman was giving out handbills with the word "Espange" on them. We concluded they must be recruiting volunteers for the Spanish war.

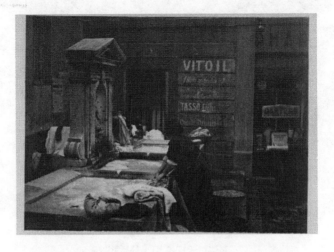

woman washing clothes in the street

Mac, Virginia, Morgan, and Colin sightseeing

market place in Marseilles

laundry hanging in the street

Virginia standing next to liquor sigh

December 12, 1936:

Our next stop was Malta, where 125 people left the ship, most of them navy men. They were taken ashore in private launches while we stood on deck with the other passengers, waving good-bye. Three new people came on board, including a man who knew some people from Dongon Hills, a section of Staten Island, where I grew up. We played the "Do you know?" game, and I have to say it was comforting to meet someone who knew where my home was. I was oh so homesick but trying to put on a good face so Ned would not be worried that I had made a mistake. I knew I loved him more each day and that I was going to be all right.

Port Said, Egypt:

When we disembarked in Egypt, we entered a different world. The men were wearing tunic dresses and fezzes.

Port Said Street, notice the policeman in fez and tunic on the corner

Street in Port Said

The marketplace was filled with new and unusual items and new smells—some of them not very pleasant. It was the first time Ned and I encountered street beggars looking for a handout. Unfortunately, it wouldn't be the last time we would be reminded of the poverty that exists here and in many other places.

We found a perfume dealer who created fragrances to suit your personality. Ned wanted me to have my own fragrance, and after some haggling, he and the dealer agreed on a price. But when he presented the final product to us, he asked for more money. Our complaints did no good. The man just shrugged and replied, "I can't help it if Madame has an expensive personality."

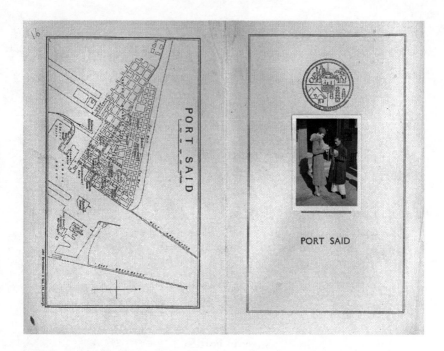

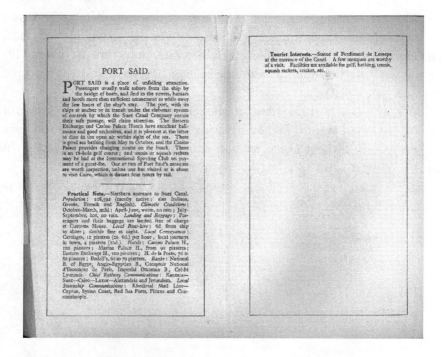

"Can't help it if Madame has expensive personality."

Port Said is the entrance to the Suez Canal. The canal was built by a Frenchman Ferdinand de Lesseps who used Egyptian slave labor to build the canal, at a great price in human lives. Many of the workers died of cholera and unsafe working conditions. The canal was opened in November 1869. The canal runs from the Mediterranean Sea and eventually reaching the Red Sea. About 120 miles long, it shortened our travel time considerably because we didn't have to sail around the entire continent of Africa. It was exciting and fascinating to see the huge ships in the canal, with waters rushing by and seeing a part of history. What a difference it had made for travel and cargo ships.

Rawalpindi in the Suez Canal

Ned, Mac, and Collin on the terrace of the Casino Hotel enjoying a drink

Clock tower on the lava cliffs above the canal

Aden, Egypt:

At the end of the canal lies Aden. Ned and I joined Colin and Mac and two new friends, Neil Oldfield and Dick Acton, for a day of sightseeing. Neil Oldfield was the nephew of Barney Oldfield, the famous race car driver. Dick and Neil were race car drivers on tour for Chrysler, headed for Singapore. Ned immediately warmed up to Neil and Dick, and I could see a friendship developing.

Virginia and Dick Acton in a rental car for a day of sightseeing

While we were in Aden, Ned and Dick donned their first *topees*. Sometimes referred to as pith helmets, *topees* are standard headgears in

Asian and African countries, designed to shade you from the sun and keep you cooler.

I wrote home that in Aden

> Saw . . . natives in costumes of all colors, greatly faded and filthy. There were no shops here at all so we went through the marketplace, which was interesting but very SMELLY. We couldn't decide whether there were more flies on the natives or the fish. The clerks were sleeping right on the tables with the fish and meat and not seeming to mind at all.
>
> Women were begging all over. They take their newborn babies along as well as three or four small children and the group follows you for blocks, murmuring in some foreign tongue to the end that they need money and you can see they do. One adorable little thing with lovely skin and eyes came up to us. She was all smiles and as cute as could be. We couldn't resist so gave her a penny. She was very excited about it and immediately took it to her mother but unfortunately several others saw the act and from then on we couldn't get rid of a mob of moaning children, no matter what we said.

Virginia and Dick with beggar children looking for a handout

Aden street scene showing the rear of a camel cart and two policemen in topees

Aden street

It was very hot and uncomfortable in Aden. I sure hoped India wouldn't be this bad. Luckily, when we went back onboard the ship, they were serving homemade ice cream. It had been ages since I'd enjoyed ice cream, and I do love it!

"Ice cream! What a wonderful treat after a hot day in Aden."

Captain Dene, a very nice chap

Virginia and Colin resting in deck chairs

Common mob soaking up the sun

Mac, relaxing in deck chair

Dick Acton and Neil Oldfield, Chrysler daredevil race car drivers

Dashing Colin Inglis

Somewhere in the Indian Ocean:

From Aden, it was off to our final destination: Bombay. Ned and I were still on our honeymoon and taking advantage of our time at sea to get to know each other better and to relax. One thing that Ned and I had going for us was that we loved to talk to each other. We could talk for hours and share all our deepest secrets, something which I think brought us closer and gave us a deeper understanding of each other.

Evenings on board ship usually brought new adventures. We had special dinners and themed parties. One night, it was a fancy costume ball, and with limited resources, Ned and I were forced to use our imaginations to come up with suitable costumes. I decided to wear a blue lace evening gown I'd brought with me and to go as "Alice Blue Gown," a popular song at the time, named after President Roosevelt's daughter. Ned borrowed a pair of overalls from Neil Oldfield, the race car driver, and a pram from one of the other passengers, and he went as "a race car driver with his own buggy." We laughed as he raced that buggy all over the ship.

There was a need for laughter at this point in the trip. The relationship between the British and American passengers had become very strained in recent days. It started when word came over the radio that King Edward

VIII had abdicated the British throne so that he could marry an American divorcee named Wallis Simpson. The news came as a very big shock to the British who hold their monarchy in high esteem. It seemed that they blamed the Americans for somehow luring Edward away from the throne. Imagine that. He was going to marry a commoner, a divorcee, and an American at that! It was a bitter pill to swallow.

Well, Ned and I weren't about to let British politics ruin the last part of our trip. We had a grand time at the ball, and two nights later, on December 23, we enjoyed a farewell dinner party appropriately named Dinner Adieu. Like all the other dinners we'd had on board ship, it was a formal affair, with men in tuxedos and women in gowns. The biggest difference now was that the men were wearing white or cream-colored tuxes, which was the custom in the East. Ned certainly looked dashing in his white tux with his beautiful blue eyes and dark wavy hair. I must say we did make a dashing couple or so we were told. "You are both so tall, handsome, and beautiful, and you make a perfect couple." I thought so too. I guess when you are in love, you radiate an aura.

After nearly a month at sea, we had made many new friends—Colin, Mac, Neil, and Dick. It was hard to think about going our separate ways, but that's what was about to happen. Some of our friends were continuing their trip across India; others were headed for families or jobs in the Far East. Sadly, we knew that we would probably never cross paths with many of them again, and this was our final farewell.

In 1936, air travel was still in its infancy; people and goods most often moved by ship. Like travel, communication was also slow. Sometimes news and letters took weeks or months to arrive. It made for a much slower pace of life. It also made it far more difficult to stay connected with family and friends.

CHAPTER SIX

India: Our New Home

Bombay, India:

Our boat docked at 4:00 p.m. on December 24, 1936. Bombay is one of India's larger cities, located on the Arabian Sea. Although India was part of the British empire, it was an ancient land of many cultures, religions, and languages. This was a place deep-rooted in history and steeped in tradition.

The country, a British colony since the 1700s, was just starting to undergo a move toward independence led by a man named Mahatma Gandhi. The process will prove to be a slow and painful one—true independence from Britain won't come until 1947.

With so many ancient customs, the country was moving ever so slowly into the twentieth century. When we got off the ship in Bombay, we felt that we had so much to learn about this exotic land. With our relationship just a little over two months old, Ned and I also still had a lot to learn about each other. Suddenly we found ourselves thrust into strange surroundings, where we would be adjusting to a life far different from anything either of us had ever known.

Fritz and Heather Elting with Dorothy Seymour

We were met at the pier by Larry and Dorothy Seymour, Paul Bunker, and Fritz and Heather Elting, all from Dodge and Seymour. Our first stop was Customs. We took the advice of the purser on board ship and lowered the declared value of our purchases in order to avoid paying a large duty. We knew it was a little lie, and I especially knew Father would never have approved. But we were on a tight budget and needed all the help we could get!

Our luggage and steamer trunks were taken to our new home by servants while we went off to the Seymours flat for afternoon tea, a British custom that had become a way of life in India. It was going to become a way of life for us as well. India and tea are one.

The Seymours flat faced the harbor, and they had a terrific view of the ocean from their terrace. It was also just a few blocks from the Gateway of India which sat next to the harbor. The Gateway had been constructed to commemorate the visit of King George V and Queen Mary in 1911. The Taj Mahal Hotel, just behind the Gateway, would soon become a favorite meeting spot for drinks and dinner.

The Gateway of India

We visited with the Seymours until 6:00 p.m., telling them all about the wonderful people we had met and all the sights we had seen in such a short time. Finally, it was time to see our new home. It was a couple of blocks from the ocean, in a boarding house called Mrs. Bentley's. The elevator was a rickety, noisy steel box that you operated yourself, pushing the lever one way to go up and the other way to go down. Sometimes it was hard to get the elevator even with the floor. But we figured it was better than having to climb four flights of stairs in the sweltering heat.

First flat in Bombay, the dining area

Ginny checking out the view

"Honeymoon suite"

Our flat was small and had a combination living room/dining area, a bedroom, a bath, and a terrace. It was furnished with just the essentials, and meals would be prepared in a central kitchen and served to us by our personal bearer with much ceremony. The rent was 450 *rupees* or about $160 per month, including all meals. Both *tiffin* and *khana* would consist of five courses and would come with all the amenities, including finger bowls. Tea would be served twice a day, if we chose to have it. My first reaction to the flat was that we had found a place to stay, but it wasn't really a home.

Our bearer or house servant was a Muslim named Kahn, passed along to us by some friends of the Eltings.

Kahn, our first bearer

Kahn wore a white turban, and we quickly learned there are many forms of headdresses in India, some plain and some fancy. You could tell a lot about a person by the type of turban he was wearing. Some turbans were of bright colors with gold edges, others had fancy folds. The different styles and colors indicated the wearer's religion, caste standing, even his native region. We were very pleased to learn that Kahn had been a trusted and well-liked servant. More importantly, he spoke English, which was definitely a good thing, considering that Ned and I did not speak Hindustani. It soon became apparent to me that I had a lot to learn about this new place we would be living in.

Our first night in Bombay, we were invited to the Eltings' flat for Christmas Eve dinner. The Eltings had their own cook and furnishings. Right away, it made me wish that Ned and I could afford our own furniture. But we were on a tight budget, and for now we would have to struggle to live on one salary and see if two could indeed live cheaply as one. I knew it wouldn't be easy, but thanks to the strong will I had inherited from Father, I was determined to give it a good try. I knew that all eyes were on me, to see just how I was going to adjust to life in India.

The meal started with tomato soup, and after a fifteen-minute break, the turkey was brought to the table. The poor bird looked like it had been shot with a cannon. The meat was hacked off the breastbone and strewn on the platter, leaving the poor thing with its legs intact and stuffing pouring out the back end. The bearer obviously had no idea how to carve a turkey.

I learned that in India, fowl is always brought to the house fresh and killed just before cooking. We were also following Indian custom and eating dinner late; it was after 9:00 p.m. when we were served. Dinner was followed by a movie—a prime source of entertainment in India in the 1930s—and then dancing at the Taj Mahal Hotel, where people were celebrating Christmas much the same way we celebrate New Year's Eve in the United States. There were party favors, hats, streamers, and noisemakers; and we had a grand time, partying into the early morning hours.

We were tired from our long journey to Bombay, but the night wasn't over yet. After the Taj, we went back to the Eltings for coffee and mincemeat tarts, and then they drove us up to Malabar Hill, an American and Parsi community where only the very wealthy live. The view of the city from there was spectacular! I thought maybe someday we would be able to live there. One can dream, can't they?

Finally, on our taxi ride home, we saw Bombay for the first time through holiday eyes. The city was very festive, with paper stars, streamers, and lights hung from many of the balconies. Besides all the Europeans and Americans celebrating Christmas, the Goanese Indians are Christians and also observe the holiday. We saw glamour and glitter that first night in Bombay, but we also saw many homeless Indians sleeping in the streets—a disturbing and unsettling sight for which both Ned and I were unprepared.

Christmas morning came too soon. It seemed we had just put our heads down when Heather arrived to take us sightseeing. Our first stop was Beach Candi, a posh private club near the water with a grand swimming pool where everyone sits under huge umbrellas and sips drinks—what a life!

Next we went to a luncheon at the Taj where we had our first taste of authentic Indian food, a delicacy called mulligatawny. A cross between soup and stew, mulligatawny is made with chicken and vegetables in a very spicy curry broth. The second course was a hot and spicy chicken curry. By this point, both Ned and I had beads of sweat on our upper lips. Thankfully, we made it through lunch with the help of some cold beers which seemed to tame the heat of the spicy food. It seemed that a good cold beer is a must with curry, just like a good red wine complements a roast.

After lunch, we sat on the balcony at the Taj and saw a crowd gather below to watch performing monkeys and a snake charmer, a common sight in India. The snake charmer starts by bringing out a snake, and after awhile, a mongoose appears. People pay to watch the mongoose and the snake fight—it's a gruesome sight as the mongoose tears apart the snake. The poor snake doesn't have a chance! As much as I dislike snakes, I hate to see such savage killing just for the amusement of the people.

Ned and I were resting in our flat, trying to absorb all the things we had seen. That same afternoon when our doorbell rang, it was the Eltings' bearer with a *chit* inviting us for drinks that evening. Very few people had phones in India in the 1930s, so *chits* were delivered back and forth by bearers. They would wait for a reply and then return to the sender with the answer.

We were both exhausted from meeting new people and seeing so many new sights that we would have liked to refuse the invitation and just spend time alone. We had not had any time to ourselves, and all we wanted to do was be together and talk about all the new things we had seen and done. But we knew that Ned was being scrutinized by his business associates, and we had to keep up appearances, so off we went.

We enjoyed drinks under the stars on the Eltings' terrace. The stars seemed so much brighter, and we saw many more shooting stars than we'd ever seen at home. With the moonlight reflected on the water and the white-painted buildings glowing, it was magnificent sitting out on the terrace. Drinks at the Eltings were followed by dinner on the balcony at the Taj. The boats reflected in the moonlit harbor made it a romantic setting.

Later I wrote home with some insight of life in India

> ... since leaving 5 Buttonwood Road. I cannot stand this English food. As Mr. Blyth said, everything is boiled until there is no taste in it. After dinner we went to see the "Big Broadcast of 1936". Very good. "My Man Godfrey" is just coming so you can see we aren't too far behind you ... just a couple of months. After the movie we came back here and we talked about running a house. I wish you could hear me. I'm almost domestic. I told Ned you would die, Mother, if you could hear me. About the first thing I did was complain how dirty the windows were as well as the front of the pictures, the glass. Do you know the covers for Collier's magazine that are drawn by Lawson Wood, usually of monkeys doing some damn fool thing? Well those are our mural decorations at present. Pictures here are terribly expensive though so we pretend they aren't so bad.

On Sunday morning, Fritz and Heather Elting picked us up and took us to the *gymkhana*—a club that both Indians and Europeans can join—for swimming, tennis, and cricket. We sat under the *shamiana* and watched a cricket match between the Indians and the British. Cricket is a national pastime in India, just like baseball in the United States. While it's played with two teams, a bat, and a ball, unfortunately, that's where the similarities between the two sports seem to end. I suppose if you understand the game it would be fascinating, but the Eltings didn't know anything about it; and of course, we didn't either, so we were bored to tears. Still, we couldn't risk offending our hosts. Ned and I put on our best faces and tried to act as though we were having the time of our lives, when all we really felt like doing was going home and putting our heads on our pillows.

The next day was an entirely different story. We were invited to the Willingdon Sports Club. It had a golf course, tennis courts, and a snooty clubhouse. We were asked to join a group of young Americans for a softball game and barbecue. The men played ball, and the women cheered them on—Ned loved the sport. A large group of Americans from different companies met every Sunday at the club located near the water, surrounded with tall palm trees. The cool breeze from the ocean made it a great place to play ball. Everyone chipped in fifty cents for hamburgers and beers, and one of the wives acted as hostess.

The food and the company were great—except for some very nervy birds called kites that invited themselves to the party. Someone was passing a tray of hamburgers when one of these large birds with talons swooped down and stole a burger. I was a little upset when one of these intruders was even bold enough to steal a bite from my burger while I was eating it!

We soon came to look forward to those Sunday morning softball games, birds and all. It was a chance to feel like Americans in a land where life was very British. It was also an opportunity to get to know other Americans in Bombay at a time when many U.S. companies were just beginning to expand their markets into India.

Ball field surrounded with majestic palm trees

"Go, team, go!"

Our first few days in Bombay had been a whirlwind of social activity and sightseeing. We met so many new people; our heads were starting to spin. But we hadn't lost sight of the fact that very soon Ned would be busy overseeing the dealers and shopkeepers who were selling Eveready flashlights and batteries all over India. As for me, I would be setting up, housekeeping, and spending time alone in this strange place for the first time since leaving New York.

CHAPTER SEVEN

Settling In

I had to admit to feeling blue when the mail came yesterday, and after nearly a month, there was still no letter from home. To top it off, Ned went to his office for the first time today, leaving me alone and lonely in this new place called home. He had not been gone very long before I was overwhelmed with homesickness. Why fight it? I sat down and had a good, long cry. A good cry sometimes does the soul a world of good.

I wasn't sure how I was going to cope in a strange place so far away from family and friends. It was 1936—our mail took weeks to arrive from the United States. And we couldn't simply pick up a phone and call home. We had no phone!

I figured the best way to cope was to hurry up and get busy. I continued to write chatty letters, being careful not to let Mother and Daddy know how homesick I was, but at the same time, constantly pleading with them and with my brothers and my best friend, Dot, to come to India for a visit.

In one letter, I tried to entice my younger brother, Gordon, and my father into making the trip by describing some odd sites and funeral customs.

> Gordon would get a big kick out of so many things here, particularly the trained monkeys and the little Chinese boys who are no older than he is and go about town doing juggling acts. The way they dispose of their dead out here is very queer. The Hindus burn their dead and you see people running through the streets carrying a stretcher on which the deceased lies. They are uncovered and bounce as they run to the burning ground.

The Mohammedans bury their dead but have elaborate
parades through town carrying the gaily decorated
casket. We passed one the other night at 12:30 which
seemed like a queer time for a funeral to me. The Parsees
put their dead in what they call the Towers of Silence,
sort of a stadium as I understand it which is very sacred
and only the priests are allowed there. The bodies are
put on slabs and the vultures eat them and the bones are
put in the sea. You can see the vultures hanging about
there a lot. Quite too lovely.

You would love the natives though, they have so
many simple and intricate turbans and sit for hours in
the oddest positions. It would be a paradise for Daddy
as far as camera material goes.

By now I was typing five-to-ten-page letters home each week. I would
usually send one letter addressed "Dearest All" and always asked my folks
to share my news with Dot and everyone else so I wouldn't have to type
five versions of the same thing. I tried to lure Dot to India by telling her
the place was crawling with young bachelors. I imagined her coming for a
visit, falling in love here, and settling down nearby. It would be heaven to
have my best friend here!

Growing up on Staten Island, our family had a wonderful maid named
Celia who was from Finland. She spoiled us when it came to keeping the
household running smoothly. Here in Bombay, I was a young bride with a
house full of servants. In India, everyone had servants. If you were poor, you
had only a few while the rich had many. This was possible because the pay
was so low that it was easy to afford servants even on the tightest of budgets.
Besides our main house servant, Kahn, we had one servant to sweep the
floors, another servant to cook meals, and still another to wash the dishes,
and another to wash our clothes.

With all this household help, I had to find something to keep me busy.
Often I would go down to the bazaar in the center of town and take in all
the sights. There were people sleeping in the streets and beggars everywhere.
If you even dared to give one beggar an anna, in minutes you would be
practically crushed by a swarm of beggars. I quickly learned not to act with
my heart, put on blinders and to just keep walking. It was heartbreaking at
first, and you had to put the feeling that you could help aside. There were so
many small children who looked like they had not had a meal in months.

The bazaar, covering many square blocks, had everything you could possibly want to buy and was set up in sections by merchandise. Food was cooked right on the street, and some of the smells were overpowering. There was rubbish and filth everywhere, also cows and *pi* dogs roamed freely. Women set up shop on the sidewalks, sometimes just placing a mat on the ground with a few dozen fruit. The *derzi* had a shop there, and you could show him a picture from a magazine, and he would copy it to fit. At six feet tall in a country of much shorter people, I would come to rely on the *derzi* for many of my outfits.

During one excursion to the bazaar, Ned and I bought a Victrola—the kind you wind up and place the needle on the record so you can listen to music. The sound was a little scratchy, but some music would be so nice, and Ned especially enjoyed hearing familiar songs. He had brought his cornet to India, but there was little opportunity for him to play.

In those early days in Bombay, Ned would come home each day for *tiffin*. I was so relieved and happy to see him that I greeted him like he had been gone for weeks instead of hours. On the days when he came bearing letters from home, I was even more excited and would quickly open them and read the news to Ned. Nearly all of India shut down during the hottest part of the day, from two to four, for tiffin and a nap. It didn't take us long to adapt to this custom. A nap was just the ticket because we went to bed in the evening after twelve, and we were up at six thirty every day.

It was New Year's Eve, and I would be entertaining for the first time. Larry and Dorothy Seymour were coming for dinner. I was very nervous and wanted to make a good impression. I had no control over the food because it was brought in from the boarding house kitchen, but I fixed up the place. I put the placemats Dot gave us on the table and fancy guest towels in the bathroom.

After dinner, we met the Eltings at the Taj to ring in the New Year. We had a grand time, and after we all sang "Auld Lang Syne," we all stood at attention and sang "God Save the King." The British, with all their pomp, must follow protocol. We partied well into the morning.

Friday was the first time we were able to sleep late. We stayed in bed and talked. When we finely got up, we opened a Christmas present from Dot, some perfume and a tea tray with little hand-painted jars of jelly. We decided that we would save the jelly for a special occasion. I gave Ned a tennis racquet, and he gave me a note that read "One dog to be delivered in the near future. Love, Ned."

CHAPTER EIGHT

Our First Taste of Life on the Road

February 1937:

After a little more than a month in India, Ned received his first assignment outside of Bombay. He would be making a sales trip to northern India, and his boss, Mr. Farrell, had given his approval for me to accompany him. I was so excited at the chance to see new sights and visit ancient temples, not to mention spend time with Ned.

Packing for the trip took several days. We had to take everything we would need, including fold-up cots, bedrolls, mosquito netting, pillows, linens, personal items, and even our own food and water. Our bearer, Kahn, would also accompany us and insisted on taking my typewriter. We were traveling as part of an entourage—Ned and I, our bearer, Kahn, and two other salesmen with their bearers, and a coolie. Honestly, we looked like an archeological expedition from the Metropolitan Museum dressed in our khakis and pith helmets. We were traveling "first class" by train from Bombay to our first stop, Ahmadabad, the birthplace of Mahatma Gandhi, India's most famous citizen. Through his efforts and passive resistance, he would fight for India's independence. The train was hot, dusty, and the compartments were very small. Ours was a little larger than the double seats on the subway in New York, and the ride was very bumpy and extremely long. We made stops at every cowshed along the way, and the natives would come out and rattle the handle and windows of our coupe, trying to sell us fruit or tea, no matter what time of day it was. It was first class in word only.

We arrived around six in the morning and went directly to the Bombay Hotel in Ahmadabad. The hotel furnishings were rustic, resembling something you might see in an army barracks. Directly outside our room was a beautiful garden filled with poppies, chrysanthemums, and roses. There were a lot of monkeys too. Just beside the hotel was a riverbed where the natives were washing their clothes.

They would slap them several times on flat rocks, and then set them on the sandy shore to dry.

India's answer to the washing machine

Veranda where the monkey decided to help me type

If you look closely, you might see the monkey up in the tree.

My scream made the troop of monkeys scatter out of sight. As I sat on the balcony that first morning in Ahmadabad, I was writing a letter home when I nearly had the daylights scared out of me. A silver-colored monkey about as big as an Airedale swung over the balcony and sat staring at me. My heart stopped for a moment. I was used to seeing monkeys behind bars but not too fond of meeting them at close range. In a letter home, I described our first hotel experience and some sights in rural India.

Ned sitting on the wall outside the hotel

Ginny's turn to sit for the camera

Dearest All:

Sleeping under the net was an experience all right but we had sprayed the bed, the curtain, ourselves, and the room with Flit so we didn't get a bite. We also have incense going most of the time too. You have to be very careful of water and we were advised to drink beer or Perrier water which we do ... At night our bearer sleeps outside our door—that is only when we are traveling of course but it seems queer. I suppose I will get used to it. He has a long knife in a case similar to the one Jack had but three times as long and when I asked him why he carried it he explained he might meet something. What he means by that I can't say because he tried to kill a lizard with it yesterday and had no luck.

... I almost forgot to tell you of the very interesting thing we saw yesterday. As you know, cows are considered very holy here and to get complete forgiveness for sins it is generally necessary to bathe in cow's urine and rub yourself with cow dung. Some natives also use the latter for fuel. Well yesterday we noticed a little girl following the cows anxiously or maybe I should say hopefully. At any rate as soon as a cow left a dropping she rushed over and scooped it up in her hands and took it to the curb where her basket was gradually filling up with it. We noticed this in several places. They make it into the form of a pancake, mix it with straw and then dry it in the sun. You frequently see huts with piles of these cakes in the front yard piled very neatly ready to burn.

Yesterday afternoon I sat in the car and watched the sights while Ned and the two salesmen visited dealers. This is certainly a man's country. Frequently I saw women pulling heavy bullock carts—the kind oxen usually pull, while their menfolk sat back in the wagon and smoked. You would be amused to see how they sell tea here. Instead of shouting that they have tea, a man takes a teacup and saucer and rattles them together with one hand in a rhythm all his own. The Indians drink a good deal of tea so they are always on the street and as soon as they get an order they run back to their shop and fill it and then start over again.

Much love to you all,
Ginny & Ned

A flit gun was a contraption that was made of a tin can with a long neck and plunger that dispensed insecticide.

Ned and the salesman Mr. Siganporia selling flashlights

Outside the shop, a sign reads Birth Control.
"It doesn't seem to be very effective."

While Ned was busy all day meeting with shopkeepers and dealers, Kahn and I often wandered through the local bazaars in these small towns, where the main attraction for me was people-watching. Kahn was excellent company—not only was he able to translate for me, but he also served as a bodyguard since it wasn't wise for a woman to wander alone through these small villages.

The bazaars were a sharp contrast to Fifth Avenue in New York, where everything is behind glass. Here in rural India, there were artisans creating beautiful things right on the street. I marveled to see young boys no older than eleven or twelve making intricate jewelry with very crude tools. I also saw women weaving silk for saris on simple, rustic hand looms.

Rajkot:

We continued our journey across northern India, arriving in a small village by way of train. This time the train was what they call a meter gauge. It runs on narrow tracks, making the train cars much narrower than usual. In fact, our sleeping cots were set out in the corridors. The windows were left open to let in air, but it also made for a very dusty and dirty ride. We were careful not to open our suitcases unless absolutely necessary, for fear that everything inside would get dirty.

Happy me.

Travel to Rajkot was extremely slow. It took us twelve hours to cover just 156 miles—so slow that we could have practically walked alongside the train and arrived at the same time. We made frequent stops so that cows could be driven off the tracks. I had to keep reminding myself that cows are considered sacred in India. It is said that it is better to run over and kill a man than to kill a cow.

We were expecting to stay in a *dak* bungalow in Rajkot, but there had been a mix-up in our reservations. A *dak* or mail bungalow was used by both travelers and mailmen who were still delivering the mail to small villages by horseback, much like our pony express of long ago. The bungalows were large structures with no windows and a hole in the roof for ventilation. Furnishings were very sparse. There were cots but no mattresses and certainly no sheets or towels. A community dining room and a kitchen was where all meals were cooked, usually chicken curry and rice or sudden death chicken, called because one minute the chicken was running around and the next it was dinner. Dessert was always baked custard which Ned really enjoyed.

Without a reservation at the *dak* bungalow in Rajkot, we were left with two choices: sleep at the railroad station retiring room or take a chance and stay at a Hindu hotel. We opted for the hotel, even though the sanitation was primitive, to say the least. The shower consisted of a drain in the floor. You simply stood over the drain and poured cold water over your body with a cup. The toilet was even cruder. It was a kind of outhouse but really just a hole in the ground set apart by two concrete slabs on either side. You simply squatted or stood and took aim. There was no toilet paper. Fortunately, we had brought some. To top off the experience, there was a servant nearby whose job it was to keep the area clean. He was forbidden to watch us as we did our business, but we were expected to throw a tip on the ground near his feet, and he would retrieve it when our backs were turned.

A very young boy who cleaned the toilet, my guess,
he was no older than six or seven.

Such was the caste system in India. It kept people employed, but since servants were expected to follow in their parents' footsteps, there was never any hope of improving their lot in life—the caste they were born into would be the caste in which they would live their whole lives and die in.

Since we would be traveling even farther into the rural countryside where there was no train service, we hired two cars in Rajkot. Once again we were loaded down with all of our bedding, food, and water and still traveling in an entourage including two other salesmen, our trusty bearer, Kahn, two *coolies*, and now two mechanics. A *coolie's* job is to do the heavy lifting, and the mechanics are along for the ride in case a tire needs to be changed. Each person is assigned one task in India and one task only.

Our car all loaded and ready to go

The two cars in the street

Two cars and a driver on the hotel grounds

One of the coolies, smiling and happy he just received
a raise to two *rupees* a month.

"The Entourage." Oh my, what a group, even one
of the hotel employees wanted in on the act.

Ned was working twelve-hour days in these little towns and villages, usually from 9:00 a.m. to 9:00 p.m., leaving me to wander the bazaars, go sightseeing, write letters home, or do some sewing. Sometimes I would sit in the car while Ned and the other salesman made their sales call, doing their best to make Eveready a household word.

One day, in one of the small towns, I was sitting in the car, and there must have been a hundred people jammed up against the car staring at me. Many of the natives had never seen a white woman, much less one who is six feet tall and wears lipstick. We truly caused a commotion nearly everywhere we went. When we drove off, they all cheered, like we were celebrities.

Gondal State Guest House, a huge improvement from the last place

Gondal was our next stop on our sales trip across northern India. I wrote home describing our brief stay there and our next destination, Jetpur:

> One thing we saw in Gondal I haven't seen before
> were religious beggars, some painted within an inch of
> their life, others in chains. They go from shop to shop
> singing and that way get money for pilgrimages. The
> cows in Gondal were different too in that their horns
> were generally decorated with brass tips, some very
> intricate work.

... We left Gondal about seven thirty to come to Jetpur. You would die to see the way they drive out here. If the road gets too rough they turn into a field and drive along the soft earth as far as they can. More fun.

When we arrived in Jetpur we learned we had been misinformed and there were no dak bungalows, in other words, no place to sleep. We did eventually learn however that there was a state guest house ... meant for high dignitaries, government officials, and any ruling maharajahs driving through. Well the sum and substance of it all is that we went to the high court Indian judge's home and he agreed to let us stay overnight in the state guest house so at the moment of this writing I am a guest of the state and I wish you could see all the pomp and splendor we are getting for nothing. Really it is an honor to be allowed to stay. We have two master bedrooms, two dressing rooms, two bathrooms, a dining room, drawing room, servants quarters, verandahs, etc .... What a life. We went up about twenty five points in our bearer's estimation when we were allowed to stay here. Such is life in India.

I was lounging at the palatial guesthouse the next afternoon, as it was far more comfortable than the car. I was enjoying a gentle breeze while I was finishing up a letter. Suddenly I spotted a small, and I do mean small, lizard on the wall, and it startled me. I called for Kahn to kill the thing to which he replied, "*Memsahib*, these are a good thing. They keep mosquitoes and flies in check." Realizing it was harmless, I worked on finishing my letter home. I had started typing when the Indian judge sent a chit asking if I would mind staying in my room while the *Maharajah* of Gondal came to the house to conduct some personal business. I couldn't get a good glimpse of what was going on, but Kahn filled me in later. He said that the *maharajah* had come to purchase jewelry and had selected a two-inch square diamond and paid seven thousand *rupees* for it, which is about $2,500.

I was learning that despite the overwhelming poverty we had witnessed, India was a very rich country. The few Indians born into the upper class and the maharajahs are extremely wealthy, many living in palaces with fine art and jewels.

Railway retiring room

The *maharajah's* wife, the *maharani*, going to her car at the train station.
She is the big black mass, actually it is a *purdah* umbrella made of scarlet red silk
with gold trim, to hide her from the public eye.

Now we were in Junagadh, Ned and his sales team were doing very well,
convincing many dealers that flashlights could be a safer light source than
oil-based lanterns. Union Carbide had the opportunity to dominate this
vast untapped market where electricity was not yet widely available.

We were also seeing village life as it had been for hundreds of years.
Women carried their babies in slings on their hips and balanced water jugs
on their heads on their way to the town well. There they would fill their
vessels with water and catch up on the town gossip. The well was also where
we saw the *dhobi* washing clothes by beating them on a rock. I could just

imagine how pretty skirts and blouses would not last long when laundered this way. They took such a beating. Pardon the pun.

The meeting place for gossip and water

Once again, we saw children collecting cow dung, although this time, we noticed that the dung was being mixed with dried grass, formed into balls, and then slapped on to walls to bake in the sun. When it is dry, it is collected and used as fuel for heating and cooking. You could tell how big the child was by the size of the handprint he or she left behind on the walls.

In Junagadh, Kahn and I hired a *tonga,* a brightly painted, horse-drawn cart with a canvas top and seats facing out of the back. The one we chose was painted turquoise. The horse was all decked out with feathers and bells, and our driver was wearing an olive green coat. It was a very colorful sight.

Tonga and driver, looking pretty dapper

Ginny, all set to go sightseeing

We were headed to the Uparkot, an ancient fort built hundreds of years ago, some think as early as the thirteenth century. There were old stone walls which had survived many wars throughout time. The old stone walls surrounded the town, built to keep out rival armies. We drove up to an old citadel from which we saw a breathtaking view of the town and Mount Girnar. The mountain is home to a Jain temple made of white marble which is easily seen but hard to get to. You are carried up in sedan chairs. We were not able to see it for ourselves as we did not have the time.

Some parts of the fort were a mass of rubble and stone while in other parts it was as if time had stood still, and the British and other invaders had not yet been there. We also explored Adi Chadi, a well built in ancient times and named after slave girls. The well had a stairway that descended hundreds of feet into pitch darkness. Kahn and I explored a mosque where we had to remove our shoes before entering to show respect for the sacred grounds. Inside there were magnificent carved doorways. Strangely, if you opened a door, it led to a wall instead of to another room. I was fascinated and awed with the opportunity to see it all. I had so much to share with Ned at the end of the day. No matter that here in India of the 1930s, we also had to endure filth, bugs, and hardship—Ned and I would not have traded our experiences for anything.

The wall and a view of Mount Girnar

Ruins within the fort

Passageway within the ruins

The stairs leading down to the Adi Chadi well

See how worn the steps are? Imagine all the people who came before me.

Another view from the wall of the Uparkot

We arrived at our next stop during wedding season, but not without some car trouble first. On the way from Jamnagar to Porbandar, the bumper of our car collapsed from the weight of all our luggage and gear. The entire job of unloading the car, securing the bumper, and then reloading the car took hours. It was done in typical Indian fashion, with much arguing about whose idea was best and which solution would work. While the servants were arguing, Ned and I sat on the side of the road in the shade trying to keep cool. We were in the part of India known as the Great Indian Desert, and it was very hot, dry, and dusty.

Looking over the situation, deciding what to do first

Now the car is unloaded. "What do we do?"

All packed and ready to go

One of the salesmen walking back to the car
after visiting with a passerby, a bullock cart driver.

When we arrived in Porbandar during the wedding season, we learned that weddings take place only after an astrologer checks the positions of the stars and planets and declares that conditions are favorable. His announcement determines the start of a short wedding season. We actually saw about five hundred wedding ceremonies during our short stay there. Wedding processions filled the streets day and night. We saw brides and grooms in cars, some on horseback, and some on foot. The guests would follow the procession on foot. The brides wore the traditional red or saffron silk saris, some sewn with gold and silver jewels, depending on the wealth of the family, and sometimes their faces were decorated with sequins. Their hands and feet were tattooed with henna. The grooms wore traditional Nehru jackets over pants that flared at the hip and tapered very snuggly down to the ankle. Their jackets were a soft shade of yellow or white and made of silk or finely woven cotton. On their heads, they wore fancy, colorful turbans, signaling their religion or their caste standing.

A wedding procession, the groom is riding in a car.

The tiny figure on the horse is the bride, a mere child.
Her face and body were covered with red sequins.

Another wedding party, the groom on horseback presided by his bride-to-be.

All is quiet for the moment in the town square.

The brides sprinkled perfume on their grooms, filling the air with a sweet aroma. Flowers were strewn everywhere. During night processions, the streets had a golden glow from all the lanterns and torches.

In India, marriages are arranged—sometimes at birth. Many times, the wedding ceremony is the first time the bride and groom see each other. Some of the girls are so young that after the ceremony, they return home to live with their families until they are older, that being ten or twelve years old. Sometimes, the brides go to live with their mothers-in-law who will train them how to be dutiful wives before they take up housekeeping with their husbands.

I wrote a long letter home about our travels from Porbandar to Jamnagar.

Monday, February 15

Dearest All,

How we do wander—here I am in Porbandar, capitol of
the state by the same name. And speaking of state, we
were again given the privilege of staying in the state
guesthouse. Guess we must have a kind face or something.
This is really very, very, ultra and surpasses the
other (guesthouse) by 100 percent. A large, large living
room complete with an oil painting of the late king of
England and one of the maharajah, etchings, books, sofa
pillows, stationery and all the trappings you never
find in such places. We have a large bedroom with a
beautiful Oriental rug on the floor and throughout the
furniture is really on the comfortable side ... Needless
to say we are taking pictures of all this splendor. But
best of all there are no mosquitoes here—at least only
a few.

While we were in a small town between Jamnagar and
Porbandar, I was surrounded by a mob of children and
adults. I was wearing slacks and after scrutinizing
me for all of ten minutes a darling little Indian boy
leaned over and said, "You man or lady?" Even the old
men and old women gather around the car and stare at
you. Very few of them have ever seen any white people
aside from illustrations. No one uses lipstick and that
causes the most amazement I think. They use bright red
caste marks on their foreheads and probably think I am
starting a new caste system or something by painting
my lips red.

Yesterday we drove from Porbandar to Jamnagar. It is
a distance of less than ninety miles but it takes the
train twenty-two hours so we came by car. Such roads
you can't possibly imagine ... No attempt is made to
build a road and one follows car tracks or drives at
random any place over the hard ground. We forded

rivers and more than once we were driving between hard clay that was so narrow we scraped both fenders at once. But you should see the ruts and bumps. We all had to buy air cushions to keep from fracturing our spines—unfortunately we had no protection to keep us from hitting the roof. At one point the baggage rack in back gave way and all our precious luggage fell directly in the path of an approaching truck. Fortunately the truck was able to stop!

Mother, I wish you could have been with me today... This morning I made inquiries about places where they embroidered saris in gold, etc. and was taken down into the slums of the town and up in the attics of some old shacks where they were embroidering in gold; Little children (ten years old) were learning the trade and getting five annas or ten cents a day. My visit created a sensation and as usual word went round and several men asked me to "honor" their shops. I saw them making cloth of gold elephant blankets for the maharajah which cost 7,000 rupees, cloth of gold rugs trimmed in pearls for some royal family, and gold and silver embroidery of all kinds from pictures to pillow covers. We could have had a marvelous time.

Ned has been working all day as usual and I expect him home soon—it is now ten thirty p.m., so I will get under the mosquito netting and wait. Take a tip from me and never marry a battery salesman if you like meals on time. Good night my loves.

P.S. Ned just came in and brought me a bottle of concentrated jasmine perfume. All is forgiven. Never marry anyone but an Eveready salesman!

"You man or lady?"

Head of the house in their white tunics and bright red turbans

Ned, Ginny, Mr. Siganporia, and Mr. Irani, enjoying breakfast on the terrace

The interior of the guest house. We had such luxuries, as a real bathroom
with running water. "What will they think of next?"

We left Porbandar for Kutch, a little country on the border of Pakistan
accessible only by boat. All passengers were asked to be on board by
midnight even though the boat would not leave the harbor until the next
morning. A carpet was laid down on the breakwater so we would not get
our feet wet, and we were escorted to our cabin by the captain. He was
quite a sight, dressed in a flowered bathrobe and bright orange turban.
To call it a cabin is actually a gross exaggeration—it was six feet square.
Imagine Ned and I—he at six feet five inches and me at six feet—cramped
in this tiny space.

When we arrived in Kutch the next day, we felt like we had traveled
back in time to the Middle Ages. The country was ruled by an old
Maharajah who also ran the silver mint; there were no banks in Kutch.
We were greeted by a grizzly looking chap standing on the dock clutching
a bag of money.

It seemed he was the banker, and he was there to exchange our *rupees*
for the country's currency.

The banker, a "grizzly looking chap"

The old *maharajah* granted permission to only a select number of people to drive cars. No drivers' licenses were required, and there was no electricity anywhere. Roads, as we know them, were nonexistent. We were met at the dock by a car and driver and quickly learned that we would be "airborne" much of the time as we navigated around this primitive area.

Dhobi washing clothes in back of the hotel

A sign above a store in Rajkot, "LONG LIVE THE H. H.THAKORE OF RAJKOT."

Women in the street

Man riding a bullock cart. The men in turbans are policemen.

Ginny and a salesman sitting on a cannon in one of the many forts they visited. The date on the cannon was 1531.

Dapper salesman and his bride

One of the many mobs that would gather around the car to gawk at the white woman

A very familiar sight: men playing cards in the street.

Soon we headed "home" to Bombay. Our month of travel throughout northern India came to an end. To save money and allow us to travel together, Ned and I gave up our first flat and moved to a new place. After just three months of marriage, we had experienced so much together in this strange but wonderful place. The time we spent together was spent getting to know each other and bond the strong love we had. We had each other's full attention as there were no other forms of amusement.

Our new flat, "Home Sweet Home"

CHAPTER NINE

A New Flat

Our new flat in Bombay was smaller than our first one, but it faced west, allowing us to catch a breeze whenever possible. And when it wasn't monsoon season, we could actually sleep outside on one of our two large terraces. An added attraction was a wood stove of our own. Kahn promised to teach me how to cook curry and rice. Rice was one dish the Indians cook to perfection. I was looking forward to adding a little variety to our diet, which often included boiled and tasteless potatoes, cauliflower, and cabbage.

We soon became friends with a young British couple, George and Ray White, who lived in a boardinghouse across the street. They worked for British Eveready and would meet us several times a week for drinks. With no telephones, we devised a unique system to contact each other. Ned would blow his cornet out the window, and they would answer by flashing a flashlight. Everyday at its best.

Ned tuning up his cornet

A view of the White's flat, the Silver End on the right
and the ocean in the background.

Our social life consisted mostly of going to the movies, playing board games, or meeting other American or British couples for drinks or dinner.

We were still enjoying our Sunday softball games at the Willingdon Club. The women would catch up on all the news from the States, sharing recipes, decorating tips, and gossip.

We all wore *topees* to protect us from the hot sun during those softball games, and you could tell a tourist from a seasoned foreigner by the way they wore their *topee*. If worn correctly, the extended brim was in the back, to protect your neck from the sun. Most tourists thought the brim was a visor and would wear it in the front. It was very amusing, and we all had a good laugh at their expense.

In the 1930s, only the very wealthy in India had the luxury of air conditioning or modern appliances. Most of the homes, shops, and businesses were kept cool with a *punkah*. If there was no electricity to run the *punkah*, then there would often be a pole with fabric hanging from the ceiling and a *punkah wallah*, whose job it was to pull a rope and make the fabric move to circulate the air. The poor chap whose job it was to keep the air moving often fall asleep, and everyone would shout, "*Punkah!*" Sometimes, he would hold the rope between his toes so his hands were free to read a book and pass the time.

Ned was working day and night to establish a market for Union Carbide products in India. Up until then, the company had been using Dodge and

Seymour as sales agents. But we both knew that Union Carbides' decision to establish its own sales offices here rested squarely on Ned's shoulders. If he and his team were successful, Dodge and Seymour would eventually be out of the picture. With Ned at the helm, I knew it was an achievable goal. He may have studied electrical engineering, but he was a super salesman, and an even better leader.

Now that we were back in Bombay, I quickly found things to keep me busy. I joined the women's club and a weekly mah jong group. I also agreed to serve on a committee responsible for dispensing funds to local charities and found time to take lessons in Hindustani.

I was definitely settling into life in Bombay, but at the same time, I was still begging my friends and family back home to make the trip to the East and also daydreaming of our trip back to New York—even it was still three years away!

In April 1937, I wrote to my family:

> Watch my dust when I get home. I am going to wear everything out before I come on leave so that I can start from scratch . . . I will start at Klines and work up town and won't stop until I reach Harlem. I have already warned Ned I will probably go haywire in each and every shop. After I finish [shopping for] myself, I will start on things to bring back for our hut. China and glass, lamps, silver, everything from soup to nuts. Just wait. Will we ever have a spree.
>
> The day after we get home I am going to Humbles [beauty salon] so tell her to be sure to stay in New York that long. We will probably be home in the spring of 1940. I want a steam bath, a facial, a pedicure, a manicure, a permanent, a cut, a set, and everything else they have from a rinse to a shampoo, to eyebrows, etc. Can hardly wait.
>
> We love you all and send heaps and heaps of love
>
> Gea

Ned was off on a sales trip again, this time to the south Indian Coast, to an area called Portuguese India. It acquired that name sometime after explorer Vasco de Gama landed there in 1498 when he set up a trading post between India and Europe. Ned was working under difficult conditions—it was hot and very humid sometimes, as hot as one hundred and nine degrees in the shade. He went to towns along the coast, Mangalore, Cochin, and Calicut. He met with success and was able to find new dealers for Union Carbide.

Railroad officer's bungalow where Ned stayed in Mangalore

The dirt road between Mangalore and Vasco De Gama

Vasco De Gama main street where "everyone but mad dogs and Englishmen are out of the noonday sun" which registered at one hundred and twelve degrees in the shade and the humidity well into the nineties.

Tongas in South India are different; the roofs are made of wood with inlaid designs and the windows have ruffled curtains.

Shampoo Indian style. Squat and lean over so water can be poured over your head with a tea pot.

Jutka stand another name for *tonga.*

A street in Cannanore, covered with woven rattan mats to keep out the hot sun. The heat here is intense.

Ned in Calicut, not looking very cool.
A bandaged knee from a fall which became infected and laid him up for a few days.

Beach Hotel cottages in Calicut facing the water.

Mr. Verghese and Mr. Acharaya, salesmen traveling with Ned.

The Malabar Hotel in Cochin built on an island.

The shop of Hajee Ebrihim Kassnm Sait, an Eveready dealer

We didn't have the money for both of us to make most of these sales trips and to keep renting our small apartment. Neither one of us liked being separated, sometimes for weeks at a time, but it seemed like there was no choice

Those long separations during our first year of marriage were very tough, but despite it all, our love grew stronger every day. While he was on the road, Ned would write me sweet letters telling me how beautiful I was and that the best day of his life was October 13, the day we had met. Often, he would come home bearing small gifts. Being apart was certainly difficult, but it only made us cherish our time together even more.

Ned wrote:

> Beach Hotel
> Calicut
> April 24, 1937
>
> My darling, darling, darling.
>
> Am very tired and miss you so much honey child. God knows I love you.
>
> I have just come in from dinner and after dinner I walked out front to watch the sea which is only a stone's throw away. The sky was very black and far out on the horizon were the lights of two ships. Not another thing except the black water, the white surf, and the thundering waves. It was very grand and how I wished you had been here so I could take you in my arms and tell you how much I love you just because you are you. Anyhow, honey child it is only 19 more days.

Ned's bosses, Ray Ferrell and Mr. MacKenzie, with his wife, were coming to Bombay, and I was meeting them for the first time. It was very important that I make a good impression for Ned's sake. It was Mr. Mackenzie who wanted to fire Ned when he asked if he could marry and bring his bride to India. There was also some concern from the higher management of the company that I would become pregnant, and Ned would not be able to support three people on a salary meant for one.

Ned, Ginny, and Mrs. MacKenzie at the hanging gardens
when she visited Bombay.

Mr. MacKenzie took Ned aside to discuss this very matter. Ned told him I was unable to have children, and our plans were to adopt a child at a later date. So we adopted the dog Ned had given me for Christmas. We named her Topsy.

Miss. Topsy our new wire-haired terrier.

Topsy was as excited as Ned.

May 1937:

So many things are changing. Our trusted and beloved servant Kahn was leaving us to go home, and care for a sick family member. Fortunately, we were able to get a new bearer, Fazel Din, who came highly recommended.

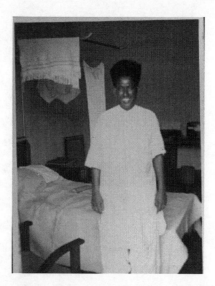

Fazel Din, always smiling, one of the best servants we ever had.

More importantly, we were moving to Calcutta to take over the office there while Ned's boss, Ray Farrell, goes on "home leave" for six months. I would be meeting Ned in Calcutta. I was left in Bombay to pack up all our belongings, and if it were not for Fazel Din, I would have been packing for weeks. He was a tremendous help. As soon as we were packed, Fazel Din, Topsy, and I made the hellish and long trip across India together.

CHAPTER TEN

Calcutta Here We Come

Train travel in India was challenging enough. Now we had added a dog to the mix! It was very hot, and again, our train had no corridors. If you want to go to the dining car, you have to wait for a scheduled stop, get off the train, and make a mad dash for the dining car, hope you are able to finish dinner before the next stop, and run back to the compartment. Naturally, we were stopping for cows along the way, getting off was not a good idea because you had no warning when the train was going to start again, and you might not be able to make it back to your car. Such was travel, Indian style.

After three weeks apart, Ned and I were finally reunited at The Great Eastern Hotel in Calcutta. As usual, we had so much catching up to do and so much to tell one another.

It is hard to describe our first impressions of Calcutta. It seems immense after Bombay and is the second largest city in the British Empire—second to London only. The shops are a lot more modern than in Bombay—from the outside at least. Europeans are not as clubby as in Bombay. There are no American associations and things like that. The streets are filled with rickshaws and very ancient and dilapidated *gharries* that look like miniature stage coaches. No European ever rides in either a rickshaw or a *ghari*, so Mr. Farrell told us in no uncertain terms. Calcutta is more of a metropolis with many nationalities represented. There is even a Chinatown. It is not as clean as Bombay in that there seem to be more cattle walking the streets, and where you find doggie's doings on New York streets; you find cow droppings on the sidewalk here. The other day when I was leaving the hairdresser's a cow was asleep directly in the doorway and I had to more or less hurdle the animal to get out.

Our first order of business in Calcutta was finding an affordable place to live. After a fruitless day of searching, Ned and I were relieved when Mr. Farrell offered to rent us his fully furnished place while he was on "home leave" for six months. It had everything, furniture, linens, books, even ashtrays. We did not have to buy a thing.

The hallway to our "new flat in Calcutta."

Ned

Trunks in the inside hall, our only place to keep them

Dining room

Living room

"honeymoon suite"

A flush toilet and running water, enjoy it while you can.

The veranda

The look says it all.

Ginny and Topsy

The stove made of cement and spray-painted bright pink

Ginny trying to cook

Ned reading *Colliers* magazine while enjoying a cold drink

Our new flat was on the fifth floor of a five-story building located right in the middle of Calcutta, on Chowringhee Street. I was so excited to finally have a kitchen of my own although it was nothing like the kitchens in America at the time. Our stove—made of concrete and spray-painted pink—had two burners but no oven. Our cook would burn corn husks, wood, or whatever was handy at the time; I'm not sure how he managed to produce meals at all with no oven and no roasting pan, but he did. As the woman of the house, I was required to see any animal before it was killed for dinner—usually chicken or duck. I was scared to death of the things, but I would go out with a know-it-all air and lift up the wings to check for scale. I had to laugh on one occasion when I caught a duck enjoying its last swim in a dishpan of suds, dishes, and all.

The cook plucking a duck

The sink in our "new" kitchen consisted of a piece of slate that drained out the window onto the rooftop below. Thankfully, we now had a refrigerator, our very first one. Now we could actually enjoy fresh food and be able to have cold drinks with ice. At last I would be able to prepare some meals for Ned, instead of eating whatever was prepared for us by the cook.

We were also given the use of a company car, a 1934 Terraplane four-door sedan.

1934 Terraplane

Our challenge would be to find money in our tight budget to keep the car filled with gas. Gasoline was very expensive—almost fifty cents an imperial gallon, compared with about nineteen cents *per* gallon at the time in the United States. Aside from trying to support two of us on a salary meant for one, Ned was also sending money home to his mother, Minn, in Canada each month.

During our early days in Calcutta, Ned returned to one of his favorite pastimes: playing bridge. Since he had pretty much mastered the finer points of the game, he was now trying to teach me how to play. It seemed as if we were eating and sleeping bridge. To be honest, I became a little tired of talking and thinking about the game during our every waking moment.

But bridge did provide us with a small circle of friends and sometimes even some gas money. Here in Calcutta, we found making new friends difficult at first. Unlike in Bombay, American and British couples didn't seem to have an organized social network, and in the beginning, nearly everyone we met was quite a bit older than we were.

Still, we joined a regular bridge game with the Irvines, an older couple we had met on the softball field in Calcutta. We also played with our landlord, Mr. Stokes, and his father-in-law, Mr. Phelps, who owned an expensive men's clothing store. Whenever we would manage to beat them at bridge, Ned and I would put our winnings into a "gas fund," so we would have a chance to use the car.

When we weren't playing bridge, we would sometimes play the Victrola and dance in our flat, or Ned would take out his cornet and play. Other times we read aloud to each other and enjoy a smoke—magazines and newspapers sent from home were always a big hit. Mother would send us *Vogue*, *The New Yorker*, *McCall's*, *Harper's Bazaar*, and *Colliers* just to name a few.

Ned was still very involved with softball, and the men played, weather permitting, every Sunday at the *maidan*. The *maidan* was located right in the middle of the city. With the Victoria Memorial, a beautiful white marble building built in 1921 as a memorial to Queen Victoria, looming at one end. It was a beautiful place with well-groomed gardens and ponds. You were hard-pressed not to be awed by its beauty.

The Victoria Memorial

Good hit, Ned. Home run!

Good catch, Ned.

"You are out!"

We also went to the movies. We were not too far behind what was showing in the States. Ned had renewed his interest in stamp collecting, which he had been doing since he was four years old. Now he had a renewed interest in collecting Indian stamps. He would write my mother, Hama, asking her to send a variety of stamps on her letters so that he would have good trading possibilities with some chaps at the office.

Life in Calcutta was becoming pretty routine. I played mah jong. We played bridge, and I spent a lot of time with my friend, Maudie Kelly, at the Calcutta Swim Club.

Maudie and Fred Kelly

Calcutta Swim Club

Maudie Kelly at the Calcutta Swim Club

Ginny at the Calcutta Swim Club

While Ray Farrell was on "home leave," Ned was put in charge of sales for India, Burma, and Ceylon. It was his first chance to prove to the higher-ups that he was capable of handling more responsibility and showing a profit—Ned was a born salesman! Our bearer, Fazel Din, was very proud because now he was working for a *Burra Sahib,*

Burra Sahib's office, Tower House. The tallest building at the time in Calcutta.

As for me, I was taking Hindustani lessons again. The language was nothing like the French I had studied in high school and proved very challenging. Ned never did master Hindustani, despite all the years he spent in India. I kept trying to learn the language, so I could communicate better with our servants.

Speaking of servants, our cook quit during our early days in Calcutta, and the new cook arrived with a helper, which I thought was a bit much. But I learned that the cook was responsible for paying his helper from his own wages and that the decision to employ him was not mine to make.

Lucky for us, Fazel Din kept an eye on all our household helps, and he would let me know when things were a miss. Before too long, he told me that the cook was padding our food bill so that he could use the extra funds to pay his helper. Since it only amounted to a few annas, I decided not to say anything.

Thunder! Lightning! Rain! Monsoon season arrived in Calcutta with a vengeance. It was like nothing Ned and I had ever seen before. At times it was so bad that the water would pick up our car and float it down the street. Cars were stalled in the streets everywhere, and people hired coolies to carry them to and from their cars so they wouldn't get their feet wet. The whole thing made me long for Bombay.

Summer 1937:

Ned and I celebrated our first birthdays together. I turned twenty-four on July 31, and he was twenty-six just a few days later on August 4. I planned to take him out to one of his favorite Chinese restaurants, and Ned surprised me with a stove. It was wonderful to finally be able to test my cooking skills. The first thing I made was cashew cookies, and I continued to try different recipes over the next several months. I really wanted to prove my skills as a pastry chef and would have loved to produce Ned's favorite, apple pie, but unfortunately, apples were about as scarce in India as palm trees are at the North Pole.

I was so excited to receive birthday presents from home too. Mother and Daddy sent me a very fashionable kelly green silk dress with a rhinestone buckled belt. It was specially made by Sophie, a family friend who was a costume designer for Metro Golden Meyer in Hollywood. My grandmother Gracie sent us a large crate—so big that Ned had to pick it up at the shipping dock. Inside was a full set of china and matching glasses. It was wonderful to have something of our own instead of using borrowed or rented dishes and furnishings.

On our nine-month wedding anniversary, Ned came home for tea one afternoon and announced that we would be taking an "anniversary" trip to Darjeeling, leaving the next day.

Dearest Mother and Daddy,

Monday and Tuesday it rained in Darjeeling so we didn't get to see Mt. Everest. In spite of it all we still claim it is the world's loveliest spot. You and daddy must be sure to see it. You can only go as far as Siliguri by train. You then take a narrow gauge train which takes five and a half hours or a car which takes two to three hours. [We opted to hire a car.] It is a magnificent drive up. Beautiful foliage, ferns, flowers and waterfalls. Once we were above the clouds and how I wished we had Daddy's filter camera to catch all the splendor. It was magnificent, particularly as it was sunset and we could see the colors spread on a cotton-like sea. The drive is a million times more breathtaking than Storm King at home yet the roads are so well cared for that one enjoys the view without feeling frightened by the heights. Of all India, it is the one place you must see.

Darjeeling did us both a lot of good. We ate like pigs and slept a lot.

Ned leaves this Saturday for Bombay and will be gone about ten days. Back to Calcutta then to Dacca for two weeks. Little Ginny will be a widow again and how I hate it. When is Dot arriving to keep me company? Just learned there is a freight line direct to Calcutta—takes three weeks and I understand it takes single girls. If by any chance she hasn't left yet and I sincerely hope she has, you might tell her to look into it.

Much, much love, Ginny

We stayed at the Darjeeling Hotel, which was accessible only by horseback or rickshaw. In fact, cars were not allowed at all in Darjeeling. The streets were very narrow and steep, and it generally took three men to operate a rickshaw, one to pull and two to push. I enjoyed my first rickshaw ride, even if it did take four men to get me up the hillside! Our trip to Darjeeling always held a special place in my heart, even many years later.

Mount Everest

Ned sitting on an old ruin with a view of Tiger Hill to the right

View of Darjeeling with the fog rolling in

Ned and Ginny outside the Darjeeling Hotel

Ginny relaxing in the room

Ginny walking in the rain, taking in all the sights at the market.

Scene of the market

A baby clinic I had never seen a children's clinic in the big cities, but one way up here, I thought it was a very peculiar sight.

"Who said women aren't as strong as men?"

Darjeeling street

Back home in Calcutta, I was anxiously awaiting my best friend Dot's visit; she was due to arrive any day now. For weeks, I planned what we would do together and who I would introduce her to. I was also constantly writing home, adding to the long list of things I hoped Dot would bring with her: toothpaste, mouthwash, eye drops, hair tonic, gingerbread mix, a drip coffeemaker, and filters—any number of things that weren't readily available in India. She was coming by steamer, so she had room to bring the kitchen sink if need.

One letter home around this time, however, had a more serious tone. I wrote about Japan's attack of China in the fall of 1937 and expressed my relief that Ned had not been sent to Shanghai as originally planned. Little did I know at the time what an important role another impending war was going to play in our future.

Ned plays *coolie*, lugging the picnic basket to the beach

Heather and Ginny smiling for the camera

Fritz and Heather napping in the shade

Ginny dons a buffalo skull she found on the beach.

At last we had some new friends in Calcutta: Jimmy and Ruth Todd. Ned and I traveled to Bombay to welcome them to their new home in India and to bring them back to Calcutta. Ned and I went to Bombay a day early so we could visit with our friends, Fritz and Heather. We spent the day at the beach catching up on all the news and just relaxing. We enjoyed a picnic lunch, and while Heather and Fritz took a nap, Ned and I went for a walk on the beach. It was such a pleasant day and so nice to spend time with old friends.

Jimmy and Ruth Todd on the train to Calcutta.

Ned and Ginny posing in the train doorway on one of the many stops
to catch a breath of fresh air.

Ned and Ginny relaxing in the compartment.

We returned to Calcutta with the Todds by train, which took several
days, giving us a chance to get well acquainted. We had lots to talk about,
and we played bridge too.

In the weeks before Dot's arrival, Ruth and I kept busy furnishing their flat with rented furniture and shopping for towels and sheets. Nothing was easy or permanent. We were never sure we would be in the same place from one week to the next. I now understood why the company only sent over single men. Constantly moving from place to place, long business trips to places with none of the convinces of home, it was hard not having the luxuries we used to take for granted back in the States.

I was also setting up a makeshift bedroom on our porch for Dot with some borrowed furniture from Mr. Phelps. I did my best to make the room homey and comfortable, hoping to entice her into staying a good long while.

Pawar playing some drums Ned bought home from one of his trips.
"Yes, he can play them."

Around this time, we had a turnover in household help. Fazel Din became very sick and went back home to try to get well. Our new bearer, Pawar, was a Hindu, and the cook was Mohammedan. I was hoping there would be no conflicts between the two. Pawar turned out to be one of the best bearers we ever had.

CHAPTER ELEVEN

Dot's Ship Arrives

Finally, the day I had long anticipated arrived.

The *Modasa* coming into the harbor

"Can you see me?" Dot was just that. Pardon the pun.

November 17, 1937

Dearest Family,

Dot's boat arrived on Tuesday afternoon and we were
there early. We spotted each other a long time before the
boat was near enough to talk to and it was awful, making
sounds and such; it seemed to take ages before we got
her on shore, and her baggage here. The bearer handled
most of that so it made it easier. Dot can't get used to
the bearer but has already learned some Hindustani
and says she will learn more. Ned has started to teach
her bridge and she says she would like to run the house
for awhile for fun. It is an entirely different process
than at home.

Wednesday we just talked and talked and talked and
then some. Gosh it is wonderful to have her here ... I am
terribly jealous of all her cute clothes, and hats and
shoes and bags so am going to have some of them copied. I
can rent a sewing machine for ten rupees and so am going
to try to make a couple myself. Dot said she would help
and believe it or not, she wants to copy one of my dresses.
Something must be wrong with the gal, but it surely is
grand having her here. I still can't realize that she will
be here when I wake up in the morning and isn't just a
vision or dream.

Soon enough we started a round of cocktail parties to introduce Dot to
our friends and all the eligible bachelors I had told her about. She quickly
became accustomed to life in India and even picked up on some of the
strange accents. One British chap spoke with such an accent, however, that
even though he was speaking English, she couldn't understand a word he
said. Still, she nodded politely as he carried on.

Before too long, Dot was going out every night with a different bachelor.
In fact, she had more dates than there were days in the week. She saw the
inside of every nightclub in Calcutta and actually received a marriage
proposal in the first couple of weeks.

November 25, 1937:

Our first wedding anniversary fell on Thanksgiving. Ned gave me a small elephant carved out of ivory and told me that he would give me a bigger elephant every year as our love grows. The trunk of the elephant would never be in a fully extended down position; Ned said because that was considered bad luck. Instead, the elephant's trunk had to be raised above the head or curled up at the tip.

He also gave me a telephone—our first phone since coming to India a year ago. Our number is Calcutta 6943. After living an entire year without a phone of our own, I was so excited. The neckties I gave Ned seemed so small in comparison. We also received a check from Mother and Daddy, which we decided to use to throw a gala Christmas party.

"Cheers!" Allen, Chick, Dot, Ned, Bud

Christmas in Calcutta was a whirlwind of social activity. We started the festivities with Christmas Eve dinner at our flat, with some friends from Ned's office. There was Allen Knapp, who was traveling around the world, Mr. Bunker and Larry Seymour from the sales office, And Chick Rourke and Bud Meeker from Ned's office. We enjoyed eggnog, compliments of Allen Knapp, and champagne, compliments of Larry Seymour. Later in the evening, the whole group of us met up with Ruth and Jimmy Todd and headed to midnight mass at the cathedral.

The white feather tree with the not-so-well—disguised sewing machine

Christmas morning, we had breakfast together and then opened presents. I was so surprised when Ned gave me a Singer sewing machine. He always seemed to know just what would please me.

Next we hurried off to the Todds for a Christmas luncheon and then back home to our flat to get ready for the gala dinner party we were planning that evening.

Dot and I had spent weeks decorating the house and planning the party. The blue and white china my grandmother sent for my birthday was our decorating inspiration. A white feather Christmas tree Dorothy Seymour had given to me when she left for the States was decorated with blue balls and tinsel, and we hung silver and blue balloons from the *punkah* in the center of the room. The tables were set with white linen placemats and had centerpieces of bachelor buttons and white candles in silver candlesticks.

We even made crackers, those small English party favors in the shape of snowballs and filled each one with little presents and specially written verses for each guest. For dinner, we served a traditional American feast: turkey with cranberry sauce, mashed potatoes, sweet potatoes, peas, onions, and creamed cauliflower, and for dessert, brownies with vanilla ice cream.

Ned and I shared this wonderful evening with six guests: Ruth and Jimmy Todd, Fred and Maudie Kelly, Dot and her date, Bus. It was almost one year to the day that we had first docked in Bombay as newlyweds, unsure of what our lives would be like in this strange country far, far away from family and friends. This Christmas, I felt so fortunate to be with the love of my life and to have my best friend, Dot, with us. The only people missing from this nearly perfect picture were Mother, Daddy, Gordon, and Jack.

Sunday, Dot slept all day trying to catch up on all the late nights and lost hours. Ned and I took this time to spend some time alone at the Botanical Gardens. It was such a beautiful and peaceful place to go and spend the day. It is one of the bright spots of Calcutta, with beautiful flowers and trees. It also boasts the largest banyan tree in the world. It was fun to picnic and enjoy the beauty of the flowers and the green grass. You almost forget the filth and dirty streets of Calcutta.

Banyan tree in the Calcutta Botanical Gardens

The lush foliage of the gardens

While Dot was there, we had a bit of a scare when we thought that Ned had suffered a heart attack. Further testing showed it to be a small hole in his heart, apparently something he was born with and thankfully nothing to be too concerned about. They recommended that he cut back on his smoking and get some rest, so we decided to take a two-week vacation to Puri, a beach town and vacation spot on the Bay of Bengal.

While we were away, the Phelps would be checking in on Dot, and Miss. Knox from Ned's office would be staying with her. Her social calendar was so full I doubt she even noticed we were gone.

There wasn't much to do in Puri—so following doctor's orders was pretty easy. We relaxed on the beach and took some bike rides by the shore. Jimmy and Ruth Todd came down to visit us on the weekend, and we also ran into Bill Ritzell, who works for Standard Oil Company and lives in Calcutta. He and Bus were roommates. Bus was the man Dot was so smitten with. Bill also thought that she was pretty special too.

Bill invited us to join him on an excursion to see the Black Pagoda, one of India's renowned temples. An architectural marvel of the thirteenth century, the Black Pagoda is carved out of black stone in the shape of a huge horse-drawn chariot carrying the sun god, Surya, across the heavens. Even in its state of partial ruin, it was quite a sight at 227 feet high. We wandered through the temple, in awe of all the intricate stone carvings. It was only after examining the carvings more closely that we realized many of them were sexually explicit scenes—a little too racy for my comfort. Embarrassed, I headed back to the car while Bill and Ned continued to explore inside the temple.

Apparently, those carvings were pretty impressive; they couldn't seem to stop talking about them all the way home. Later, I learned they were drawings based on the Kama Sutra. On the ride home we did make a short stop when we spotted a huge anthill, as tall as I am, on the side of the road. We emerged from the car to take a closer look, but when Bill told us that big snakes in the area are attracted to the ants, Ned and I quickly hopped back in the car. A short distance down the road, our car ran over a large black cobra, so apparently Bill knew what he was talking about.

Back home in Calcutta, Dot and I spent time catching up on all the news and sewing up a storm. We made a nightgown and bathrobe to match and a couple of dresses. We were also playing a lot of tennis, since some of our friends lived in houses with their own tennis courts and big beautiful gardens.

Ned, after a game of tennis

Ginny and Topsy, both pretty good at chasing the balls

I hoped we would live in our own house someday soon. Apartment life was very confining, especially when the flat was in the middle of Calcutta, and on the busiest street in the city.

Cows on Chowringhee Street, the main street of downtown Calcutta

Dot was pretty smitten with Bus. I was so anxious to know if he was "the one," but it was too soon to tell for sure. Practically every man who met her was taken with her, and why not? She's a very pretty young lady, and had so much to offer.

Change was in the air again. Mr. Farrell, Ned's boss, had returned from "home leave," which meant we had to move out of his flat and get a new assignment. Sadly, Dot won't be able to stay on with us since we're not sure where we would be living; and after five months, she started to run low on funds and couldn't afford a hotel.

April 24, 1938

Dearest Family,

Dot left Saturday night and I never felt bluer in
my life. Spent most of Saturday and Sunday weeping in
fits and starts. Gosh but it was ideal having her here
and she surely was the perfect guest. The house seems
so empty without someone to talk to all the while. Life
out here is nice but most of the time I'd give it up for
just a week at home.

There were nine of us to see her off and we all
took flower garlands. She went up to Delhi and Agra
and then goes to Bombay. I've written Heather and Mrs.
Bunker and Bud Meeker are over there now so she won't
be lonesome.

Dot is bringing you a present from me, Mother. Two
very old and what I think are very lovely figures from
China or Japan which I bought in Bombay and planned
to use as bookends but never did ... She is also bringing
Gordon a pair of real Indian drums which Ned bought
up country. They are the ones the natives all use out
here.

Ned is due so I'll stop. All sorts of love to all of you
and tell Toots for me that I sure miss her daughter like
hell. We did have such good times together. I still can't
realize she has really left.

Much, much love and many thanks for the dotted swiss
and the sweat shirts. I love you.

                                                        Gea

May 1938:

Ned and I were assigned to Madras where he had been named branch
manager of the new operation there. It was a nice step up the ladder for him
and showed that all his hard work had not gone unnoticed.

We had hoped to leave Calcutta by boat, traveling down the coastline,
but unfortunately, we weren't able to make accommodations at the last

minute, so we had to take the train. You know how much I love the trains in India. Our friends gave us a marvelous sendoff at the train station. Fred and Maudie Kelly, Ruth and Jimmy Todd, the Phelps, Chick Rourke, Ray Farrell, Bus Putnam, Fritz Elting, and our bearer, they were all there to shower us with small gifts—everything from gum to eau de cologne.

As usual, our two-day train trip was hot and filthy; Ned and I were accompanied by Topsy, our dog, and Ned's assistant, Bill Reynolds. He would be traveling with us, and he would be working with Ned in Madras. Bill would be making some of those sales trips up country, which meant that Ned wouldn't have to travel so often. It pleased me that he was going to be able to spend more time with me. I missed him so when he had to travel.

The Connemara Hotel

When we first arrived in Madras, we took up residence in the Connemara Hotel. We were told by Ned's boss that now that he was moving up in the company, we would be expected to keep up appearances. That meant buying our own car, joining a club, and looking for a flat that was on the "right side of the tracks," unlike our place in Calcutta.

For now, we were finding it difficult to live in a hotel, especially with our dog. We also had to contend with formal dinners at the hotel that required us to dress up each evening.

To top it off, Ned had another health scare while we were staying at the Connemara. He developed a fever of 103 degrees, and the doctors said he might be battling malaria, dengue, or typhoid. Fortunately, his blood work showed that it was none of these, but I sure was anxious for him to get well. In between battling the fever, he had chills, so all the *punkahs* had to be turned off, and it was hotter than hell in our room. Besides, he just wasn't a very good patient. Thank goodness after a few days of bed rest, his fever disappeared as mysteriously as it had arrived, and he was ready to return to work.

CHAPTER TWELVE

Madras: Ned's Hard Work Pays Off

Our new house was on Kilpauk Garden Road, in a section of Madras known as Babington Gardens. It was one of several houses grouped together around a garden and a tennis court. The house was rather picturesque, with green shutters and a red tile roof, and made out of mud that had been whitewashed. It had no glass in the windows but rather had shutters that could be closed during a rainstorm. It was a two-story house, more spacious than anything we've had so far despite all the drawback. There was no kitchen to speak of, and we had sold our stove when we left Calcutta. Then there was the water issue. Madras had a water shortage, so our water was rationed. We were able to get cold water only twice a day: in the morning until ten and again in the evening from six to ten. If you want a hot bath, the water has to be heated outside and then carried into the house in buckets. As you can imagine, our bathroom facilities here were primitive. They consisted of a potty chair, and of course, there was a sweeper who would come in and clean up after us because there was no running water to flush.

Our first house. New to us but far from new!

A view of the house and the surrounding gardens

Ginny relaxing in the shade, "Boy, is it HOT here."

It was very difficult to furnish our house in Madras. Curtains and rugs had to be made special, and finding decent furniture to rent at a reasonable price was also a challenge. Even hanging a picture was a major undertaking. First we had to remove a chunk of mud from the walls and fill the hole with a piece of wood. Then we had to fill around the wood with plaster, paint it white, and wait for it to dry. Finally, we could hammer a nail into the wood to hang a picture.

Ned had a little better luck finding a car. After some serious shopping, he purchased a four-door 1935 Ford sedan with a built-in trunk.

The car getting a free wash, thanks to the monsoon.

Overall, it was a challenge to adjust to Madras. If we thought Calcutta was hot, Madras, being farther south, was even hotter. It wasn't unusual for temperatures to reach 108 to 110 degrees in the summer. It also felt like we had traveled backward in time. Compared to Bombay and Calcutta, Madras was a quiet town with very little going on, and during our early days there, I missed my friends and our weekly mahjong and bridge games.

Before too long, Ned returned to Calcutta for a sales conference. As he was packing, I decided to hide little love letters all through his luggage in his underwear, his shaving bowl, his suit pockets, and his pajamas. It would be a small reminder of just how much I missed him when he was away.

I needed to keep busy, so I started to work on planting a garden that would bloom in December. It seemed a little backwards to me to be thinking about flowers that would bloom in the winter. But here, the summers were too hot and dry for much of anything to grow.

I was also told that we would need at least eight servants to run our household, although at first that number seemed high to me. Eventually, we did end up with eight: our bearer, a *chokra*, two sweepers, one for the inside of the house and one for the outside, a cook, a *dhobi*, a *mali*, and now a servant to clean the car. It would be years after we left India before this caste system that designated only one task per person would start to change.

June 25, 1938

Dearest Family,

Ned had to leave day before yesterday for a flying trip to Calcutta—some sort of a sales conference of all the branch managers so I am doing my best by my lonesome here in Madras.

Our house is gradually getting furnished and the garden planted . . . Incidentally, did I tell you I have a gardenia tree in my compound just loaded with flowers—takes me back to Fifth Avenue and the little old women on the corners. Naturally ours aren't the hot house variety but still in all they are very super gardenias and I fill the house with them.

Have found two girls who are nearly my age so the town improves. A Lois Perry who is an English girl married to the branch manager for Goodyear Tires here and Eileen Lippincott who is the wife of the American vice consul and Daddy will be glad to know that Aubrey Lippincott, Eileen's husband, is a Beta Theta Pi . . . He used to work for the Bell Telephone in Arizona at one time and was very much interested to hear my pop was a Beta and worked for Telephone too. Guess that makes you all brothers under the skin.

Played bridge once last week and also mah jong. Can't even go to the movies in this town, they are so rotten; Can't hear the voices and the carbons are so miserable you can't see the people half the time. What a jumping off place this is. Wish Celia could see the stove my cook uses. There isn't even an oven so he bought a clay bowl about two feet wide and a foot deep and it is set on three legs. He puts charcoal on the floor under this and then covers it with a lid arrangement and puts charcoal on top of that and there you have the oven and believe it or not he makes delicious soufflés in it. I can't understand it all.

Well my little ones, heaps and heaps of love from me to you and then some.

United Battery Distributors Ltd.,
Seated: Mr. T. S. S. Rao; Miss. E. Everett; Mr. J. E. Potts, manager;
Mr. W. G. Reynolds, asst. manager; Mr. A. F. Morass; and Mr. R. S. Doral
Standing: Mr. S. M. Venkatachalam; Mr. P. V. Verghese;
Mr. K. A. Srinivassan; and Mr. V. E. D'Cruz

Finally the big day arrived when a new Union Carbide company took over the reigns from Dodge and Seymour sales agents. All of Ned's long hours and hard work had paid off. The new company was called United Battery Distributors Limited. I was so proud that Ned's office was number one in sales in all of India.

I could hardly believe we were celebrating our second anniversary, and Ned had given me another ivory elephant just a little bigger than the first. He said it showed how our love had grown. I am so happy I followed my heart.

CHAPTER THIRTEEN

Letters Home From the Road

Negapatam
December 11, 1938

Dearest Family,

Please forgive the pencil but you see we are on tour and when I say on tour I really mean it. No electricity at all so thank heavens the weather is coolish. Every time I try to eat or read by these kerosene lamps I want to send Mr. Edison a note of thanks. Speaking of modern conveniences, I can hardly wait to get back to the U.S.A. and drink the water from a faucet and get hot water from the same source. This business of giving the gardener notice three hours before you want a bath is not so good in my estimation.

Speaking of baths though—the first morning we arrived here we sent the bearer out for hot water to wash with. He came back with a grin on his face and reported that they wanted to charge him six annas (about 15 cents) for water in the kitchen so he went to the fireman on a locomotive and got it from the engine boiler free. He has been getting it from the engines for three days so we'll probably begin to smell like them soon.

In case you are in doubt as to why there are engines about, let me explain that we are staying in the railroad station's retiring room—a crude room and bath (no running water) where we can stay for about a dollar per couple per day. Aside from Dak or traveler's bungalows these are the only accommodations to be had on tour.

This place is absolute heaven though in comparison to our first night in Cuddalore. The traveler's bungalow was full and there were no rooms at the station so it meant the car or the Y.M.C.A. which was filthy and lacked sanitation of any kind. Literally not a john in the place nor any way to get food or any beds—merely bare rooms. We went to the station three and a half miles away for our meals and used their bathroom but believe you me I surely wished I was a man then. When there is no drinking water and you drink beer instead it takes legislative planning to be at the station when you need to be. Do I make myself clear?

We're having loads of fun. Ned plans to tour a lot during January, February and March so will see South India for sure. Everything is green and totally different from the scenery in Kathiawar. Many rice fields and palm trees.

Yesterday we were in Nagore and saw the famous Mohammedan Mosque there. From here we go to Tirunelveli and Tiruchirapalli and then Madura—arriving there a week from today which will make a tour of two weeks. Then we are back to Madras.

Well my loves that is all for now. I love you loads—less than a year and we'll be saying it instead of writing it.

Gea

Masque tower in Nagore

Town square in Nagore

Travelers' house in Kumbakoam. "Looks nice enough from the outside but cockroach-infested inside."

A pool of water where the villagers can go to wash their cloths and bathe.

Falls at Tanjore said to have healing powers

A very pleasant place for Ned and I to have a picnic,
enjoy the falls, and a reprieve from the heat

We spent the day at the town of Madura, one of the oldest in India. There we found a very large temple devoted to the Hindu god Shiva. The complex is one of the largest Hindu temples and dates back more than two thousand years, making it one of the oldest too. The temple complex is surrounded by a tall wall with four *gopuras* at each corner and seven more in the interior of the complex. The *gopuras* have a solid granite base, and they range in height from one hundred to one hundred seventy feet tall. It is covered with stucco figures of mythical animals, monsters, and deities. We wandered through the complex which had many halls, great rooms, shops, and animal stalls, where the temple elephants were housed. The smell was most unpleasant. The tank of holy water had steps leading down so that devotees could bathe. There were lots of halls and rooms to explore—the Hall of the Eight Shakti, the Court of a Thousand Pillars, each one more elaborate than the other. The pillars had ornate carvings that were spectacular. The place was a great source of knowledge about the Hindu religion. Ned and I were able to get a real sense of what the Hindu faith was all about. We were there during one of the religious festivals and saw a great cart. It was one huge piece of wood, completely covered in great detail. The wheels were seven feet wide with huge nail heads. The whole thing was very impressive. The cart is used to take Shiva from the main temple to another temple three miles from the city with a huge tank where Shiva is bathed in the holy water. It was all fascinating, and we were glad to be in the right place at the right time.

Main door to the Great Temple of Madura

One of the twelve *gopuras* which are within the temple and the tank of holy water

Hall of the Eight Shakti, named after eight goddesses carved in each pillar

Statue of Shiva at the corner of the tank

Religious procession, a camel covered in gold cloth and festooned with jewels

Worshipers carrying a likeness of Shiva covered with a canopy
to protect him from the sun

A temple elephant covered with gold cloth and jewels

Another elephant. "What is a procession without elephants?"

The temple band and other worshipers

The gigantic cart, one huge piece of wood

A close up shot of the carving on the cart

The huge wheels

The tank and temple three miles out of town where Shiva
is taken for a holy bath

Boxing Day is a big celebration in India. Boxing Day is a British holiday celebrated on December 26, when gifts are opened and shared with those less fortunate. Now that Ned was a *Burra Sahib*, we were showered with gifts from the dealers, office coolies, and shipping agents. They came to our door with flower garlands, baskets filled with fruit, a bottle of whiskey, and delicious fruitcake.

With the generous Christmas check from my parents, we decided to join the *Gymkhana* Club in Madras, giving us a place to meet friends and swim. While I really wanted to call my family in New York on Christmas Day, I strongly resisted the urge to place the call because we were in the midst of a "saving drive." Having a house, many servants, and a car was a strain on our budget.

Around this time, I was invited to tiffin at the home of a Mrs. Mott, the aunt of Mother's best friend, Bess, back in New York. It truly is a small world! Here I met a woman by the name of Marie Buck, who would eventually change my view of life in India.

January 2, 1939

Dearest Family,

The big red letter day as far as I was concerned last week was Friday. The day I had tiffin at Mrs. Buck's and met Bess' aunt. I drove up at twelve-thirty and Mrs. Buck, someone I had never met, rushed out and helped me put the car in a spot that would be shady and Mrs. Mott met me on the doorstep with a big kiss. She is really a darling and I did my best to put my right foot forward.

She showed me pictures of all her family and we chatted away at a great rate. Just to show you how much of an occasion I considered it, let me add that I wore my new hat, the only time I have had a hat on my head for almost a year.

We talked until luncheon time about this and that. Dr. Mott was still busy at the conference so I was not able to meet him unfortunately but from everyone's account he is a marvel. It was marvelous getting with someone who talked about something besides clothes, food, drink, or bridge and mah jong.

Mrs. Buck is very active in welfare work and said she wanted me to help her. I think she meant it too. He is a Y.M.C.A. Physical Education man—by far the nicest couple I have met in Madras.

I can't think of much to tell you about Mrs. Mott except that she is a darling person . . . exactly the kind of person you wish was related to you instead of just an acquaintance. She showed me your letter, Mother, and took a couple of kisses from me to you. Thank Bess too for me because it was really the nicest day I have spent in Madras.

Well my loves it is time for me to take a bath. Ned is taking me to see Robin Hood at six tonight. Everyone says it is an excellent film. Be sure and thank Bess for me and tell her I think her aunt is absolutely tops. Much love to you from me and I'll be seeing you ere long, my little ones.

Marie and Crowe Buck

Ned and I were traveling again, this time to southern India, including Calicut, Cochin, Coimbatore, Trichur, and Oatacamund. Touring in this area was often monotonous. I had a *Murray's Guide to India*, but here in these small towns there were no attractions or sights whatsoever. I would sit in the car or walk through the bazaars while Ned made sales calls. Very often I would become the center of attention, with hundreds of people crowding around me, coughing in my face, making cracks to each other, and laughing. Sometimes I felt very uncomfortable and most defiantly out of place.

"You looking at me?"

During this trip, we saw the results of a drought since there had been no rain in the region for a year. It was over one hundred degrees, and people had no water to drink. Even though they still had food, if the rains didn't come soon, it would mean no harvest this year, which would lead to famine. The people seemed sadly resigned to their situation, believing that "what will happen, will happen."

The women of the village would walk for miles to get water. When there was none, they would leave their water jugs in a line in order of their arrival and come back later in the day when the water pressure was better.

Despite it all, I still loved touring with Ned—but shorter trips were best as far as I was concerned. As for Ned, he was so smitten with wanderlust that he was talking about giving up our house in Madras and buying a station wagon, having it fitted with water filters and portable beds. He would be content to live on the road! I, on the other hand, liked the comforts of home, even though they were few. While we were in Cochin, the SS *Rawalpindi* (the ship on which we'd sailed into Bombay) came into the harbor. We weren't able to go aboard, but it was nice to see it just the same.

Our next stop was Trivandrum. Not much to see, but there was a nice zoo. It was the first time a European visitor had been to the zoo, and the owner was so proud to show off his animals. We were able to pet a tiger cub and a baby elephant. It was the first time Ned and I had been so close to wild animals. At first I was very wary of being so close to wild animals but soon saw they were so small and harmless.

Ginny with a tiger cub

Just after this shot was taken, the baby elephant sneezed and scared me to death.

On our way from Trivandrum to Cochin, we also saw a typical example of Indian efficiency. The Trivandrum government was expecting a visit from the viceroy and had decided they would build a bridge in his honor. They hired thousands of coolies and worked them day and night because they only had fifteen days to erect this hundred-foot span bridge.

All went well until the day before the viceroy was due to arrive. They had finished the bridge and were just getting ready to test it by having a car drive over the bridge, when suddenly the whole thing collapsed into the water. Well, they immediately started to work building a new bridge. Such was life in India!

The pontoon ferry that we used to get across the river

Fortunately we took a picture of the finished bridge before the collapse.

Without a doubt, the highlight of our tour was a stop in Cape Comorin, a very romantic and scenic place at the southernmost tip of India. Here, Ned and I stood on a high, rocky peninsula and saw a spectacular sunrise over the Bay of Bengal in the east. That evening, we shared a beautiful sunset over the deep azure Arabian Sea to the west, while to the south was the Indian Ocean, reaching all the way to the South Pole.

We took a leisurely walk, hand in hand on the beach, crossing this entire tip of India from east to west. Now we could tell our grandchildren that we had actually walked across India—never mind that it was a distance of less than one mile!

For me, Cape Comorin rivaled Darjeeling in breathtaking beauty. I hated to leave, but we had to continue our trip up the west coast to a region called Malabar. Known as the "garden spot of India," Malabar was full of lush green vegetation like no other place we had seen in India. It stood out in sharp contrast to the dry, dusty towns we had visited earlier. In Malabar, waterways carve canals deep into the jungle all the way up to the Ghats Mountains where they grow tea, coffee, rubber trees, cashews, cardamom, and other spices. The crops are so abundant that the area is rich in agricultural exports.

A view of the road coming into the cape

Travelers' bungalow in Cape Comorin on the beach and right next to the water

The swimming pool was filled with crabs, so no swimming for us.

All the conveniences of home. A potty chair just like the one
we have at home, with armrest and a box of sawdust.

A view of the bungalow annex, and off towards the water, the *Maharajah* of Travancore's house at sunrise. The sunrise was spectacular enough to get us up and out of bed. You know that it had to be to get the two of us up so early.

The southernmost spot in India, the Bay of Bengal on one side, and the Arabian Ocean on the other. You could stand on the beach and see both bodies of water simultaneously.

Ginny sitting on a very crude boat, a few logs held together
with rope and a prayer.

Alleppey Harbor, a very picturesque place

Travelers' bungalow looks can be deceiving. It was filthy inside.

I am enjoying drinks in Cochin with Mr. Verghese and an Eveready dealer, Mr. Venkatachalam Rangaswami Chettiar. "The only letter left out of his name is a *z*."

CHAPTER FOURTEEN

Back Home at Last But Not for Long

Back home in Madras, we were practically melting from the unbearable heat. The reports claimed it was 106, but it felt closer to 150 degrees. The clothes in our closets were hot when you put them on; our sheets were burning; the silver on the table was too hot to touch; and the little wind we had was like a blast from an oven. And to think that they were predicting ten more days of this.

The good news was that Ned met with his boss, Mr. Farrell, and he was full of praise for the outstanding job that Ned and his assistant Bill were doing. The even better news was that Mr. Farrell said we would be going on "home leave" in November. I was so excited I could hardly sit still.

Ned and I had already mapped out our return trip. We planned to go home by way of the Orient, taking a boat from Calcutta to Rangoon, then on to Singapore, Shanghai, and then Kobe and Yokohama, Japan, next to Honolulu, then Vancouver, Canada, and finally taking the Central Pacific Railroad to New York. Little did we realize at the time that our travel plans would change practically every day due to the havoc the war was having on Europe and Asia. Traveling was becoming very risky.

We had also begun to talk about adopting a baby while we were home. We knew that our chances of adopting a white baby were far better in the United States or Canada than they were in India.

It seemed that there was hardly a dull moment in our household in Madras. Around this time I received a *chit* from an anonymous person telling me that one of our servants had syphilis. We had no idea who it was, so we sent them all for a Wasserman test.

On top of that, our cook was testing my patience. If I asked him to serve fish, he would serve duck. I guess his theory was that they both swim!

One night, Ned and I were just sitting down to dinner when we heard an ear-splitting crack, followed by a moment of silence and then the sound of crashing timber. A mango tree, about five feet around, had come crashing down in our yard, taking with it our telephone wires, my garden, and two concrete posts. Within minutes, it seemed like all of India was climbing through the debris in our yard, collecting the ripe mangoes. People and monkeys alike were scrambling for the fruit which is eaten raw or made into chutney which is served with curry.

One of our neighbors invited me to his home to witness an unusual practice among the Moslems to mourn the death of a prophet. I watched in disbelief as hundreds of men stripped to their waists and then began flailing their chests with their fists so hard that their skin began to blister and bleed.

It seemed that our lives at this time were a study in contrasts. One day we were playing tennis, going to the movies, and hosting dinner parties. And the next day, we might be off to the backwoods of India, trying to figure out where our water and food would come from.

June 11, 1939
Dearest Family,

Robinson Crusoe hadn't a patch on us as far as this trip goes and I begin to think that Byrd is a sissy compared to the trials of touring this section. We left Madras about six on Friday morning, picked up the salesman and his coolie and headed for the wilderness. Our first stop was Chittoor—the mango district. After tiffin of mutton curry and rice which should have been called leather curry and rice, Ned went to the bazaar and convinced a few dealers that Eveready batteries last longer. That night we drove eighteen miles to a railway station in Katpadi for some tomato soup, some Cross and Blackwell potato salad, a tin of Libby's Vienna sausages and a tin of peaches.

The next day] we had hoped to get tiffin in Manamaduri but there were no dishes or cutlery to be had so we sat on the bungalow steps and opened our tin of beans, sardines and peaches. We bent the top of the bean tin and used that for a spoon and let me tell you it is quite a knack to eat beans from a tin top without slicing your mouth several times. We are past masters now.

We have been cooling our water by putting the bottle in a wet towel and swinging it from a tree for half an hour. Really gets quite cold. Nothing quite like necessity being the mother of invention.

Arrived in Kurnool about five thirty and had tea and are settled in for a few days. Ned took a bath (all tin tubs up here and believe you when Ned tries to collapse his height in one it is better than a circus). At any rate the bathroom was alive with ants—huge black ones. We complained to the manager and he said it was all right, they would leave in a short while. Next thing we found was a scorpion about five inches long which we killed by throwing lighted matches and burning toilet paper and eventually a rock. Incidentally, an hour after we killed him, he had been devoured by ants who returned for the feast.

At this point I heard a moan from the bearer. He was just bitten by a scorpion and we tourniqueted his arm but he is convinced he will probably die. Don't think I like this town.

Friday—

Left Kurnool this morning after breakfast and I for one wasn't sorry. Just as a side line—they kept the pepper on the table in a Pond's cold cream jar. Ned says this is the worst trip we will make and I believe him. The bearer has recovered from his scorpion bite.

No letter from you this week Mother but the American and World Fair booklets were forwarded to us and were certainly appreciated. Many many thanks and much much love.

Ginny trying to eat a can of cold beans with the lid.
The trick is not to cut yourself.

July 14, 1939

My Dear Little Tiddlewinks:

This is your healthy ox speaking from the back woods station known as Rajahmundry. A town with one European bank manager and a sixty-year-old Swedish American woman doctor from Rockford Illinois and her European assistant. And how glad I am for the latter two personages.

Ned went to bed in good health and spirits on Monday evening and woke me at three a complete wreck. He was chilled to the marrow and shaking like jello and his head was burning up. I covered him with everything available from sweaters to bath towels to no avail so at six I woke up the salesman in the next room and we went to the bazaar to wake up a chemist and get a thermometer.

At six thirty his temperature was 103 and I was plenty worried. We eventually learned about the doctor at the mission hospital outside of town and I rushed out there and brought her back. She was very comforting and gave him half a dozen medicines to bring the fever down. It went as low as 102 but no more and terrific diarrhea set in. I was all for putting him in the nursing home here but he refused so he took more medicine and next day he was almost normal. He stayed in bed until this morning and now feels pretty fit and we go on tomorrow. He is drinking three and four glasses of Hollicks daily and doesn't seem to be weak. I wonder what would have happened if I hadn't decided to come along at the last minute on this trip. What a life we do lead.

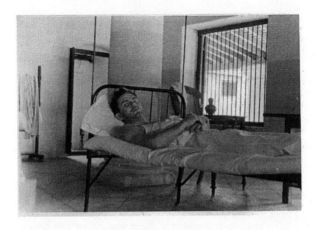

Ned, looking a little feverish

Travelers' bungalow I call "Malaria Mansion"

Railway station interior. People sleep and cook on the floor.

Outside of the railway station is their version of the hotdog cart, serving cold drinks, tea, fruit, *roti*, and curry.

"Yes, she is naked from the waist up." A very common sight.

We arrived home in Madras to find our house in shambles. Not only had the house not been cleaned for weeks, but there was food and beer left out on the tables, and some of our things were broken. None of the servants seemed to know how this happened. I'm growing tired of the bugs, the heat, and the filth. Some days India was so fascinating and full of new adventures, but I was longing more than ever for the comforts of Staten Island.

There were no paved streets in Madras, even the main street was dirt.
Coolies are leveling the surface.

An elephant with a temple cast walking in the street

Women gathered on the edge of town, waiting for the bus to the villages

A very tall ceremonial cart being taken down the street

A funeral procession with the deceased on a stretcher being carried
down to the burning *ghats*

A policeman under a cement umbrella directing traffic
on the main street in Madras

A mounted guard on his horse with lance in hand, looking very sharp

Indian garbage wagon

Victoria Technical Institute in Madras

CHAPTER FIFTEEN

War News Was Bad News

We inherited a broken radio from one of our neighbors, and with a little fiddling, Ned was able to get it playing again. We could receive broadcasts from all over the world, even Canada. What a treat it was, even if the news we were getting these days was frightening.

Hitler's army was now marching across Europe, and it seemed that there was chaos everywhere. Japan had invaded China, and there was no telling what would happen next. We knew one thing: We would not be visiting the Orient on our way home. In fact, we might not even be heading home.

One minute it seemed like the war in Europe was far away, and the next minute, it was in our backyard. We returned home from a friend's house one night to find the police visiting our next-door neighbors, Fred and Anne Rauleder, a German couple, and their three-year-old daughter. They gave Mr. Rauleder twenty minutes to pack his things before taking him away to an internment camp.

Anne Rauleder was naturally very distraught, so I spent the night with her, trying to assure her that it would be all right. We spent the next few days packing her belongings for storage and moving her and the baby into the YWCA, where they would await the government's decision regarding women and children.

Anne Rauleder and her daughter Rene

Fred Rauleder and daughter

It was so heart-wrenching to watch her trying to decide what to store and what to sell. She would run her hand lovingly over a table and say she hated to sell it because it was her husband's first birthday present to her. Or she would examine a set of china and say she hated to sell it because she and her husband picked it out on their honeymoon.

The bitterest blow came when she hadn't finished packing yet and her belongings were being auctioned. Perfect strangers just swarmed in and started to pick through all her things, even the baby's toys. I felt an overwhelming sadness.

War was declared in Poland on September 1, 1939. Ned decided that he didn't want to visit his mother in Canada only to risk being drafted into war in Europe. He told Mr. Farrell that he would prefer to stay in India, and I could either go to south India or home to the United States. I had no intention of going anywhere and leaving Ned behind.

In a letter home on September 9, 1939, I wrote:

> Sea travel is far from safe these days as witness the Athenia so unless it is a short war we won't be home for Christmas. Both of us feel badly about it. The firm is willing to pay my way home but I would certainly hate to get home and then be forced to stay there for four or five years with Ned out here in India. An ordinance has been passed making it necessary for Ned to register with the British army here and it is doubtful he could leave now even if he wanted to. He hasn't been told to report as yet but many men are now on twenty-four hour duty guarding such places as gasoline installations, harbor entrances and so forth . . .
>
> Air mail has been reduced from five services a week to one and the rates have been more than doubled. Your letter of August 17th did not reach me until a day or so ago and was censored as is all mail not going to or coming from some part of the British empire. I have both a British and an American passport so can seek protection from either in case of trouble so there is no need for alarm. It did seem funny though to think of some stranger opening and censoring your letter to me. In order to speed up my letters to you I am sending them all to Mrs. Potts [Ned's mother in Canada] and asking her to forward them immediately. In this way they will not be censored and will receive preferential treatment. She will be glad to forward your letters as well if you want to send them that way.

Around this time, we were maintaining a close relationship with Marie Buck, the woman involved in social work who I'd met at Mrs. Mott's house a while back. Ned and I started going to Marie's house several nights a week to listen to the American broadcasts, and sometimes she would telephone us to report important developments in the war.

A group of us also became involved, rolling bandages for the Red Cross. We were asked to featherstitch some kind of fancy bandage that was used on injured backs, but I wasn't very good at it. At least I was trying to do my small part for the war effort.

September 1939:

Word came to us from the corporate office in New York that Ned and I should try to leave India on a neutral ship as soon as possible. We immediately went into high gear trying to find a ship that could accommodate us.

Most of the steamers were fully booked, but there were two possibilities: we could take the Dollar Line *President Polk* through the Mediterranean or possibly a P&O Liner by way of Australia.

Before we had a chance to book either ship, however, we saw an ordinance in the local newspaper prohibiting all male British subjects from leaving India without permission from the district army headquarters. Ned immediately wrote to headquarters asking for permission, and we sat and waited for a reply.

By this time, my head was spinning with plans. If they denied his request, we would both stay in India. If they let him go home, it wouldn't be wise for us to go to Canada because there was a chance the government could conscript him into service while there.

I imagined that we would spend the full six months of "home leave" in New York and that Ned's mother, Minn, would have to travel there and stay with us. We couldn't possibly all stay at my folks' house on Staten Island, so I was busy hatching a plan to rent a cheap apartment somewhere on the island.

Finally the day arrived when we were given permission to set sail for home. We left Bombay on October 21 aboard the SS *President Polk* and were due to arrive in New York on or about the twenty-third of November, just in time for Thanksgiving. I was so excited I could hardly think straight!

I had written ahead, asking if my parents would host a small group of fellow travelers and friends for Thanksgiving dinner, including Eileen Lippincott and her young son, Gordon, and two fellows from Standard Oil. One of them was Bill Ritzell who still had a thing for my best friend, Dot, and had gone so far as to tell me he would marry her someday. Since Dot was in love with his roommate, Bus, I told him I thought he was crazy and didn't have a chance.

Ned aboard ship.

Ginny, finally on her way home

CHAPTER SIXTEEN

Back in the Good Old U.S.A.

November 25, 1939:

Home at last! Ned and I arrived safely in New York, exactly three years to the day we had first left. How wonderful it was to enjoy a real Thanksgiving with our family and friends. My folks, Hama and John, my brothers, Jack and Gordon, my best friend, Dot, and Bill Ritzell were all there; and our cook, Celia, made a Thanksgiving feast. The best thing was the turkey was tender and juicy, and Ned had his favorite apple pie.

Next on my agenda was to get my hair done by our favorite salon owner, Mrs. Humbles. I hadn't had a decent cut or set since our wedding three years ago. I was so disappointed to learn that Mrs. Humbles was in Europe, so her assistant would have to do.

From there, it was on to a shopping spree on Fifth Avenue. Most of my clothes were at least three years old, and since they had been laundered by a *dhobi* in India, many were faded and worn, not in good shape at all. Besides clothes, we needed shoes and many household items that just weren't available in India.

Our six months at home flew by. We spent Christmas on Staten Island with my family, and after much deliberation, we decided it was safe to travel to Canada to spend Easter with Ned's mother, Minn. We also took time to visit Ned's best friend and college roommate, Buster, and his wife, Peggy. We had a lot of catching up to do. We also visited with his cousins, George and Betty Faulkner, and his uncle Burt.

There sure was a lot of snow on Easter Sunday

The house in Stirling where Ned grew up.

Bus and Peggy with their son Brian. He was Ned's college roommate,
and Peggy grew up with Ned.

Although it was spring in Canada, there was a lot of snow, and it was still
very cold. It was such a drastic change in weather from the oppressive heat
of India. It was frosty cold and snowy. We enjoyed the snow; we were like a
couple of kids playing in the snow for the first time, even venturing out to
build a snowman. After six months of visiting with family, shopping, and
relaxing, it was time to return to India. With the war going on, we knew it
wasn't going to be an easy trip.

Ray Farrell, Ned's boss, was in New York, and we enjoyed a night out
on the town. "What a hat."

The family, Gracie Potter, Hama's mother, Hama, Ginny, John, and Ginny's young brother, Gordon.

The Empire State Building in the fog.

We had a difficult and tearful good-bye with our family and friends in New York before heading by train to Minnesota to visit with my cousins, Pattie and Georgie, my uncle Phil, and grandma Ray. From there, it was off to Los Angeles to see Sophie, a family friend and dressmaker for the stars. While we were there, she made me an exquisite suit. Ned was full of compliments, telling me how beautiful I was and how the suit made me look like a million bucks. Ned was always telling me that I looked beautiful and that he loved me so very much. We were so happy and still in love, looking forward to a long and happy life together.

Next we were off to San Francisco where we would be taking a ship home. It seemed strange to think of India as home, but it was the place where Ned and I had built our life together.

According to Ned, I looked pretty sharp in my new suit Sophie
had made for me.

May 1940:

We set sail for India on board the SS *Bloemfontein*, a ship of Holland registry, one of the few passenger ships still sailing to the East. Since Holland was a neutral country, this was our safest choice.

The *Bloemfontein* was a large ship, but there were very few passengers aboard. With Japan waging war in China and Indochina and Hitler warring in Denmark, Norway, Belgium, and France, there was a travel advisory against unnecessary travel to the East.

Aside from Ned and I, there were eight officers, the captain, and only four other passengers on board, including two missionaries, Rev. and Mrs. Gordon Jury, who were going to Burma, and Mr. and Mrs. James Hanlon, some old friends of ours who were traveling to Calcutta with us. And this was a ship designed to carry one hundred passengers!

Jim and Betty Hanlon, old friends from Calcutta, also returning from "home leave." He worked for Standard Oil Co.

The ship's officers told us that when we were able to pronounce the steamship line's name correctly, then we would know Dutch. With a name like NV Vereenigde Nederlandsche Scheepvaartmaatschappij (United Netherlands Navigation Company), Ned and I believed them.

We made a short stop in Honolulu, Hawaii, where we were welcomed with traditional leis, and we had some time to sightsee and enjoy lunch at the Royal Hawaiian Hotel. Then it was back on board where it would be another two weeks before we would see land again.

Ned and Ginny standing on the pier in Honolulu,
in the background is the Aloha Tower.

Hula dancers in the park

While we were at sea, the frightening news came that the Germans had invaded Holland, and the country was now under German occupation. We were no longer on a neutral ship. With warships out to sink nearly anything that floated, our captain decided to set a course that would corkscrew to our next port. This maneuver made the ship roll even on the calmest of seas.

Thankfully, our accommodations on board the ship were very comfortable. We spent our days playing bridge and table football, swimming, and organizing treasure hunts, and occasionally, we would have great water fights in the empty corridors. I had also bought a huge crossword puzzle in San Francisco, and nearly everyone on board took a turn working on it.

Afternoon tea, relaxing after a hard day of play.

Playing table football, Jim and Ned against Gordon and a crew member.

Huge crossword puzzle with over four thousand words

On the more serious side, Ned and Jim Hanlon were given the task of camouflaging the ship. All the windows had to be covered with tape, and we could not use lights of any kind from sunset to sunrise since we were observing a "blackout." In one of the ports, they even painted the ship gray, so it was harder to see from the air. The risk of Japanese war planes shooting at us was a very real concern.

Ginny knitting to pass the long hours. Notice the taped windows.

The ship's steward putting up shutters to protect the windows.

Jim applying paste to strips made from navigation maps
because they did not have enough tape for the windows.

Painting the ship gray so it was harder to spot from the air.

This turned out to be a long and worrisome trip. We spent nearly every evening with the crew huddled around the radio, listening to grim news broadcasted from Germany and England. Hitler sounded like he wanted to rule the world; his invasion into most of Europe and nightly bombing raids on England were terrifying, and the Japanese were now fighting in the Pacific. Our Dutch crewmen were very worried that their family members might be raped or killed. The news was grim, and the threat of war all around us.

Our ship made many stops, but we were only allowed to disembark on a few of them, one being Manila Harbor. Ned and I had dinner with friends there, but the atmosphere in Manila was tense. The harbor was filled with battleships and submarines, a sure sign that the war was not far away. We weren't allowed to take any pictures, and nearly everywhere we looked, there were censors or police. Our world suddenly felt like a very dangerous place.

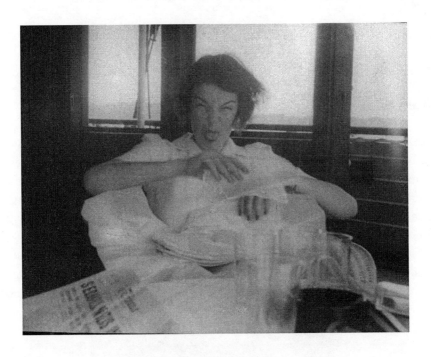

Ginny expressing herself "ENOUGH."

CHAPTER SEVENTEEN

Back in India, Safe and Sound

June 1940:

We had been reassigned to Calcutta. Ned and I were counting our blessings to have made it safely to solid ground. Nearly every day, we hear stories of some acquaintances that were not so lucky. Some were lost at sea, others were stranded in lifeboats for days, and still others were whisked away to concentration camps; and to make matters worse, the Japanese were moving troops closer to India.

For our second stint in Calcutta, we were able to rent a big house in Ballygunge, a part of Calcutta just outside the city. Our new home at Five Rainy Park was a beautiful two-story house with its own garden and tennis courts.

Five Rainy Park, the front entrance

The grounds

Our servants

Ned and I, the Potts, were living on the ground floor, and the Waters an English couple living above us. I joked that all we needed now were the Dranes. Strangely enough, a few years later, we would share a house at Two Rainy Park with an Australian couple Edna and Jack Drane.

The war was wreaking havoc on our mail delivery. Our letters home were being censored, and we never knew when a ship would be sailing with mail to or from the United States. It was now taking months to get news from home.

If we weren't getting frequent letters from home, at least we had company here in Calcutta. Marge and Jim Shafer, another couple with Union Carbide, were staying with us until they could find a place to live. Marge and I were able to get along very well, and together we became busy furnishing the house.

I screamed with joy the day news arrived from home that my best friend, Dot, and Bill Ritzell—yes, the same Bill who vowed he would marry her before she even gave him a second look—were indeed planning to tie the knot. I was so happy for both of them but disappointed that we couldn't be in New York for the wedding.

Closer to home in Calcutta, Marge and I were busy planning another wedding. After mounds of paperwork and telegrams back and forth, one of Ned's coworkers, Dwight Wait, had received permission to bring his bride-to-be to India. Dwight and Alice were to be wed in our beautiful garden, which our upstairs neighbor Mrs. Waters tended with great care.

We had beautiful date palms with orchids around them, poinsettia hedges, and hibiscus in every shade imaginable—really a beautiful setting for a wedding reception. Well, Alice arrived on the *President Polk* on schedule, but as luck would have it, her trunk didn't arrive with her. Now mind you that she and Dwight were to be married the same day she arrived. With her luggage somewhere out there, she had nothing to wear for her 5:00 p.m. wedding.

Marge and I quickly went to work to dress this poor girl who had been a model for a big store in Cleveland and who had packed a beautiful gown, not to mention an heirloom hankie and a precious locket for her "just so" wedding. Marge loaned her a white pique formal dress, and I offered her a white bolero to cover her shoulders, and the wedding came off beautifully, if a little differently than Alice had originally planned. Welcome to life in India! After the wedding, Dwight and Alice went off to Darjeeling for their honeymoon.

Marge and Alice arriving at the cathedral

Alice and Dwight made their grand entrance as Mr. and Mrs. Wait.

Dwight and Alice the adventure is just beginning.

Dwight's brother, sister-in-law, Mary, married to Herman Wait.
Standing behind them is Andy Gormely

Mary, Dwight, Alice, Herman, Ed and Ruth Melton, Jack Zerbst,
and Reg Hughes

The happy couple cutting the cake

Ned and I have joined the globe-trotters again. We rouse at 3:00 a.m.
one morning, and by 4:00 a.m., we were on our way to Benares, the sacred
city. It was only a journey of about four hundred miles, but it took us almost
twenty-one hours. It really shouldn't have taken so long; however, when we
arrived at the town of Mughai Sarai, about ten miles from Benares, we had
to wait four hours before we could get across the famous Ganges because
the pontoon bridge was washed out. That meant we had to put our car on

a train to cross the river. Our itinerary on this trip included Jupur, Agra, Lucknow, and Allahabad.

Our bearer, Ali

Ned waiting and waiting

Ginny in the car and Ali standing guard as the train leaves for Banaras.

Ned and Ginny resting on the car bumper on their way to Allahabad.

The happy couple on the veranda at the hotel in Allahabad.

December 18, 1940

Dearest Family,

Well here we are back in Cawnpore on our way home—we are like horses—once we are on the home stretch we rush for the stables... We have had a marvelous trip. The past two weeks have been an interlude neither of us will ever forget. We did a bit of sightseeing in Delhi after seeing the fort. The Qutb Minar to be exact which is a tremendous mosque.

Also went to the Ivory Palace in Delhi, Mother, and looked at bridges of ivory elephants. The ones they had at about one hundred dollars were stinking affairs with poor carving... I got discouraged and said to show me the very best one they had in the shop. With much ceremony they produced a velvet box the size of a casket lined with satin and showed us a huge tusk carved in one piece. It was really lovely but actually not half as nice as we had hoped and they wanted ten thousand rupees. I told them to wrap it and send it C.O.D. as I knew you would like it. You had better leave the tag on it though so people can see your three thousand dollar hunk of animal tusk...I really hope you like it because that is a lot of money to put in a trinket like that.

We had two days in Agra and spent most of the time sightseeing and still felt we had only scratched the surface of things. Naturally we saw the Taj Mahal by moonlight first. The first glimpse is priceless and one compares it with a cloud, an earthly moon. You really can't put words together to describe it—it describes itself in marble. If you saw nothing but the Taj Mahal, a trip to India would be worth it.

Heaps and heaps of love to you all.

Ned and Ginny at the Taj Mahal. The scaffolding put up to protect the dome in case of an attack by the Japanese.

Ginny at the Taj Mahal, one of the seven wonders of the world.
A truly beautiful place.

The Tower at the Qutb Minar, the tallest brick minaret in the world

The Iron Pillar, a pillar that was made in ancient times and is located near the tower. It is said if you can stand with your back to the pillar and reach back around the pillar and touch your hands you will have good fortune.
"I guess being so tall gives me an advantage."

Ned following suit.

Pearl Mosque. What a magnificent place.

The Red Fort in Delhi

Humayun's Tomb

An old door and the old man keeping watch. So many horse shoes nailed to it.
We were not able to get an answer as to the reason for the collection,
but we thought it was a great photo.

An old Indian with his water bag slung over the shoulder. The bag is made out of goat skin, similar to the European wine skin but much larger.
Close at hand, he was never too far from his hookah.

We had a new addition to our household around this time. We gave Topsy to friends when we went on "home leave," so we decided to get another dog, another wire-haired terrier like Topsy. This time, a male, and we named him Micky. He was quite the show dog. I entered him in dog shows in Calcutta, and he won first place more than once.

Micky was a great show dog

Ned was working very hard to straighten out some problems in the Calcutta office. First, he was down by one salesman when our houseguest, Jim Shafer, became quite ill with dengue fever and was eventually moved to what the Indians call a nursing home and what we call a hospital.

There were also several salesmen in Ned's office who were not pulling their weight and who needed to be let go or placed on probation. Aside from that, when Ned took over the office, there was a tug-of-war going on between the head office for Eveready in India and the Calcutta branch. He would eventually get that sorted out but not without a lot of frustration on his part.

Fortunately, the New York management team recognized Ned's efforts to get the Calcutta office fully staffed and to deal with all the headaches. They realized that, unlike many others who had come to India as salesmen and management, Ned was able to meet any challenge that came his way. While the company wasn't quick to increase his salary, they did provide him with a car and driver and even sent him a bonus. We were also benefiting from the lower value of the *rupee*, our American dollars were now able to buy more in India. With the war raging in Europe, our "good fortune" was about to change.

Calcutta Office Team and Their Wives, 1940
Seated left to right: secretary, Miss. Delanuserade, Ruth Melton, Marge Shafer, Ginny Potts, Mary Wait, Edna Drane, Alice Wait, secretaries Miss. Stewart, Miss. Percell. Standing: Mr. Elkin, Ed Melton, Herman Wait, Andy Gormely, Jack Zerbst, Mr. Stewart, Pete Orr, Dwight Wait, Jack Drane, Reg Hughes.
Third row: Ned Potts, Ken Brooks, Tom Riley

CHAPTER EIGHTEEN

The Army Comes Calling

April 1941:

Ned received word that he may be called to serve in the British army. His boss, Ray Farrell, had designated him a "key" person in the office and tried to make the case that he was indispensable to the company, but apparently there was a pressing need for college-educated officers. We began a waiting game about our future in India. If Ned was drafted to serve here, I would stay with him, but if he was sent overseas, I would be heading back to the United States. Neither one of us even wanted to think about the idea of being separated.

I was keeping busy, both with a social life that included dinner parties and afternoon teas, bridge and tennis games but now also making time to help out more with the war effort and with Indian charities.

I volunteered at the Women's Home Companion, a store that sold handcrafts made by Indian women. I also joined the Women's Club of Calcutta and put my typing skills to use as their secretary. The club was holding bake sales and bridge tournaments to raise money for the war effort, and I was baking date-nut bread by the carload. I was also still rolling bandages for the Red Cross.

Ned and I had certainly enjoyed the freedom of having our own car and driver, but now there was no gas available to keep the Ford running, and we had to resort to riding bicycles or taking trolleys to get around Calcutta.

We were also being forced to observe curfews and blackouts. The blackouts—which meant no electricity after sundown—were the worst, especially in the unbearable heat.

July 31, 1941:

It was my twenty-eighth birthday, and Ned surprised me with a big, beautiful sapphire and diamond ring. It really was so divine! He had not been able to afford a ring when we became engaged, but he always promised me that as soon as he could, he would buy me a ring. This wonderful man was true to his word! I could hardly resist the temptation to show it off every chance I had.

The managers were in Calcutta for a meeting, and of course they played ball.
"A pretty motley crew if you ask me."

September 1941:

After months of tense waiting and speculation, Ned finally received his orders from the army. He was given a commission in India as Lieutenant Colonel. His official job title was assistant civil engineer advisor to the deputy director of factory expansion-explosive division of armaments production in the Department of Supply for the governor of India. In layman's terms, he would be fighting fires for the Indian government and running the factory making explosives for the troops.

Ned in his "army uniform"

Ned was very distressed that he was being forced to take a leave of absence from his job, all because he was a Canadian citizen and in fact a British subject. He was hardly consoled to learn that he was guaranteed to get his job back when the war was over. He felt that he had worked so hard to move up the corporate ladder and that his induction in the army would quickly take him down a few rungs. What's more, he feared that in his absence, someone would step in and fill his shoes, and he would be left far behind.

There was little we could do to change the situation, so we simply had to accept it. The war had already changed so many lives, and now it was changing ours. We were both relieved that he would be serving in India after all and wouldn't be sent overseas. It meant that we could keep our house and stay together for the time being. The thought of life without Ned by my side made me shudder. I loved him so much that any thought of separation made me too sad.

Many companies were going out of business or leaving India, including the Dodge and Seymour, the export agency. The war had made it impossible to trade and move raw materials. With so many restrictions on imports, companies that did not have factories in India were quickly being put out of business.

Japan had just invaded Burma, and the fear was that India would be next. We were getting word that some of our friends in Manila and Burma had been killed or were in concentration camps.

December 7, 1941:

Japan bombed Pearl Harbor, and the United States had declared war on Japan. Less than a week later, on December 11, Germany and Italy would declare war on the United States. There was no doubt we were in the middle of another world war.

December 11, 1941

Dearest Family,

Heaven only knows how mails will go now that Japan has entered the struggle. Isn't the world in a sorry, sorry mess.

It has been announced that the officials anticipate sporadic air raids in Calcutta within a month. We have laid in an emergency supply of food so there is absolutely no need for you to worry as our home is situated far from any possible target or missed target. In an emergency, naturally the cable office will be mobbed. We will make every effort to get word through as quickly as possible so please try not to worry. In case of attack all women will be evacuated to the hills. I know you are bound to worry but think how much more fortunate we are here than we would have been in China or Java or someplace right in the thick of it.

Everyone seems to have awakened to war responsibilities. Yesterday I was asked if I wanted to be in a Firefighter's canteen. I don't know whether to do that or try for a job as messenger or ambulance or truck driver. I know I want to do something.

Last Sunday I organized a magazine collection for the troops. I was able to get the Ford Company to donate a couple of trucks and sent circulars to all the Americans in Calcutta and we went around picking them up. We collected about six big cases full and a few days later we had a nice letter from the Y.M.C.A. thanking me for the effort.

I don't like to rub it in but after Daddy's letter a year ago I just like to prove to him now and then that I'm not decaying too speedily—because I (did) such a good job handling the personnel of the American Tamasha, they have asked me to do it again for the fete to be held at the Viceroy's house in January. Really no honor and just a lot of work, but then at least they asked me.

Charlotta Sinclair and her husband left for Rangoon shortly before Christmas and gave us their living room furniture to keep while they were away; they had a lovely beige rug and several nice pieces so we look simply beautiful and completely furnished! Heaven knows I don't envy her life in Rangoon. Now they have had so many raids there Calcutta is getting on edge and all the Indians and their families are closing their shops and going to their village up country. Pretty soon we will probably all be doing our own housework.

I have just finished an A.R.P. course in the method for putting out incendiaries, etc. It was very interesting and I haven't a doubt but what we will be raided before too long. Japan radio promised it to us some time the latter part of this month but so far they haven't kept their word. I have trained all my servants in the proper precautions and we have practice air raids now and then.

If Rangoon is taken, Ned will send me to South India he says but I think it would be better to stay here instead of twiddling my fingers there and wondering what is happening.

Our news is so censored that there is no telling what side of the picture we don't know. I repeat that if Calcutta has a bad raid we will try to cable but we have been told the cable offices will probably be closed for business for the first few days so you must go on the assumption that no news is good news and if the raids are frequent, naturally we won't cable after each one.

CHAPTER NINETEEN

That Dreaded Day: Orders for Evacuation

1942:

We had never been so happy to see monsoon season arrive! For now, it was helping to keep the Japanese at bay. The mountains were covered with thick fog, making it impossible for aircrafts to fly in. This was in the days before pressurized airplanes, when the planes simply couldn't get enough altitude to clear the fog over the mountains.

Ned was working long days for the Indian army. He had to report at 9:00 a.m. and was on duty until 9:00 p.m. each evening. With a blackout still in effect, he had to make his way home on the tram at night, walking the last mile or so from the station. Sometimes I would arrange to get a bicycle sent to the home of a friend of ours, and he would ride the last stretch home. Either way, I worried until he made it safely through the door.

I was volunteering at the YMCA a couple of times a week. They couldn't afford to pay me, but I figured at least I was keeping my shorthand and typing skills up to date. They also fed me pretty well, providing coffee, lunch, and a heavy tea at 4:00 p.m. every day.

There was a lot of discussion around this time about women being evacuated before the air raids came—but we learned from Washington that there was no air transportation available and no ships of any kind being sent our way anytime soon. So our plan remained that we would simply head for the hills if the raids came, or if there wasn't time for that, we would hide in our "slit trench." Everyone was building these trenches, ours was roomy enough for sixty people; it had a concrete floor and galvanized sides, drainage, and a roof. We had planted grass on top to hide it.

April 1942:

The day both Ned and I had hoped would never come had arrived: The United States government ordered the evacuation of all women and children from India. I was forced to travel back to New York while Ned stayed to fulfill his duty with the Indian army.

Before too long, our house was turned into a makeshift camp for soldiers. We had twenty cots set up in our living room. While I was part of a small group of American women preparing to leave the country, we had British friends who were not allowed to go back because England was being bombed daily by the Germans, and India was the safer of the two places. They simply headed for the hills up north and hoped for the best.

Our hearts were breaking when the time came for Ned and me to say good-bye. When we reached the train station in Calcutta, I couldn't hold back my tears any longer. Ned was trying hard to be reassuring. "This won't last long," he said. "Before you know it, we will be together again." But as we gave each other one long last embrace and a kiss, he was fighting back tears too. We really didn't know how long it would be before we would see each other again—it could be months or it could be years. I didn't even want to think about Ned being in harm's way if the Japanese started bombing India.

There were so many things we didn't know about our future when we said our tearful good-bye that day in Calcutta. But one thing we knew for sure: our love for each other was stronger than it had ever been.

I was sobbing my heart out as the train pulled away from the station in Calcutta. Not only was I leaving Ned behind, but I was now on my own to make my way back to the United States in very dangerous and uncertain times.

My traveling companions were Marge Shaffer and Margaret Buckman. Marge's husband, Jim, who was well again, was staying in India to work for Union Carbide, since the office was short of manpower now that some of the men—Ned included—had been drafted.

Margaret told us that her husband was Chinese, and he wasn't allowed to leave China. As a foreigner there, she had endured many hardships.

Marge looked at her and asked, "If you had to do it over again, would you still marry a Chinaman?" Margaret looked stunned. Taken aback, she replied, "I didn't marry a Chinaman I married the man I love." I think that short conversation drove home to all three of us just how much the war was straining relationships. It didn't matter which nationality you were; there were bumps in the road ahead for all of us, and we needed to support each other.

From Calcutta, we traveled by train to Karachi. Here we had been invited to stay at the house of a friend, a Mr. Vandusen, who worked for Standard Oil. He had room to spare since his own family had already been evacuated. In fact, we joined a group of people, some of them old friends, including Alice Wait, Eloise Rourke, and Fran Goldrick, who were also taking advantage of Mr. Vandusen's hospitality. When we arrived, we learned that each day the women would go to the airport in Karachi to try to get a flight out of the country. However, there was only one flight a day on a small plane that held thirty passengers, so progress was slow.

Air travel in the 1940s was far different than it is today. At the time, planes were not designed for passenger comforts such as meals. Meals were not served on board. They were served when the plane landed at the terminal. The terminal was sometimes a little shack or even a big tin hanger, not the luxury of today's terminals. Once we succeeded in getting a flight, it meant we would be hopping from one small city to another, stopping often to refuel and grab a bite to eat whenever we could.

It actually would have been quicker and much more comfortable to travel home to the United States by ship—but unfortunately, all the ships had been activated for war duty and to say nothing of the perils of war at sea.

While I was stranded in Karachi, Ned and I stayed in touch by phone when possible, but more often we sent telegrams. He would send me short cables reminding me of his love: No matter what time of day or night.

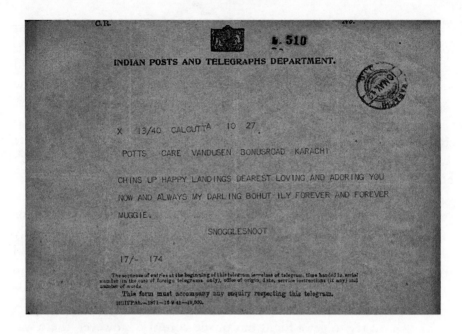

Bahut-ily (pronounced "boat-illy"). *Bahut* is the Hindi word for
"very much." And *ily* is short for "I Love You." It was our way of saying,
"I love you very much" (our own secret code).

Alice Wait was one of the lucky ones. Her husband, Dwight, had been
transferred to South Africa, and she was given permission to meet him there.
So she went back to Bombay and caught a ship sailing to South Africa.

As for me, I made daily trips to the flight office in Karachi for six solid
weeks before I was finally given permission to board a flight. By this time,
I was tired and relieved to finally start my journey to my family in New
York.

Fran Goldrick would be my traveling companion. As Fran and I
waited at the airport for departure, no one was more surprised than I when
world-renowned aviator Jimmy Doolittle approached me and presented me
with an orchid corsage. Aside from making aviation history several times in
the past twenty or so years, Jimmy had recently received the Medal of Honor
for successfully leading a precision bombing raid on Tokyo.

It seemed that Ned had met Jimmy in Calcutta, and in a casual
conversation, Jimmy mentioned he was headed back to Karachi where a lot
of the Flying Tigers were stationed. That's when Ned had the idea to ask
him to present me with the corsage.

In fact, Jimmy and most of the Flying Tigers were well acquainted with the ladies in Karachi waiting to catch a flight home. The group had actually formed a small club called the Short Snorters Club. Membership was by invitation only. The friend who asked you to join would hand you a dollar bill with her signature on it. From then on, you had to carry that dollar bill with you at all times, and if you were ever caught in a bar without your dollar bill by another member, you had to buy a round for everyone. I had received my dollar bill from Marge and would carry it with me for years.

CHAPTER TWENTY

My First Time on a Plane

I was both excited and terrified as Fran and I prepared to board our flight out of Karachi. This would be my first time on an airplane. As it turned out, our plane was a big airship designed to take off and land in the water. It was like a two-story bus, with two levels of seats facing each other. It felt like we were in a theater, looking down at the other passengers. I was a little apprehensive to learn we were headed to Cairo, Egypt—not exactly away from all the fighting. During take-off, water rushed by the windows, and it seemed as if we were underwater, not on top of it. One of our stops during the trip was in Haifa, a city on the coast of Israel famous for its oranges. As we disembarked from the plane, which was very hot, we were all so thirsty. How happy we were to see a pitcher of fresh orange juice waiting for us at the restaurant where our meal was being served, but our relief quickly turned to disappointment as we watched one of the men from our flight drink the entire pitcher of orange juice by himself. Back on board the plane, we hit some turbulence, and you guessed it—the poor man was airsick. His seat was in the upper balcony, and the passengers below him were in for a huge surprise! The man was obviously embarrassed and tried to make apologies to everyone, but with little or no insulation in the plane, the engine roar was so loud that no one could really hear him. Two days later, we finally arrived in Cairo; once the Nile River had been cleared of all boats and traffic, we could land. I was so relieved that our long, hot, and noisy plane ride was over—but I wasn't really sure what lay ahead.

Many of the passengers—Fran and I included—opted to stay at a place called Shepard's Hotel. If you had to be stranded in Egypt in the 1940s, it was really a nice place to stay. While there, I reconnected with some other friends from India, Ed and Ruth Melton, who had arrived ahead of us.

One of the first things I did after arriving in Cairo and at each stop after that was to send Ned a telegram to let him know where I was and that I was safe. He would cable me back care of the flight office so I was sure to get his messages.

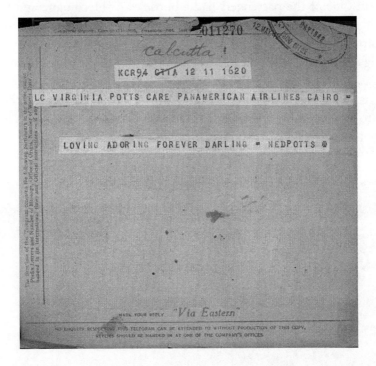

My traveling companions and I spent two weeks in Cairo, sightseeing and trying to get a flight out of the country. Finally, we were scheduled to fly to Lagos, Nigeria. This time we would be flying on a DC-3 troop transporter. There were no real seats on the plane; we had to sit in metal boxes designed for men wearing parachutes. The parachute was placed in the box and used as a cushion. Without a parachute or a cushion, it wasn't very comfortable at all. It was the only time in my life I wished I had more meat on my rear end. What's more, the plane had no windows, only gun turrets which let in the smallest bit of air. The plane was not pressurized or insulated and was so noisy that there was absolutely no way to carry on a conversation of any kind.

When we stopped to refuel in the middle of the desert outside Khartoum, a large city in the Sudan, we were allowed to get off the plane for a short breath of fresh air, but it was so hot. It really wasn't very pleasant at all. The fuel came from a stockpile we had been carrying on board. I wasn't too keen on the idea. What if the landing was not so smooth? The fuel was poured into the tank with a funnel and a shammy cloth as a filter. The desert sun burning down on the plane had grown even hotter during our short refueling stop. Getting back on board, we felt like we were walking into an oven. One of the passengers had a bottle of 4711 cologne and to help cool off, we decided to douse our arms with it and then put them out the gun turrets. As the alcohol in the cologne evaporated, we enjoyed a short cooling sensation. Our food during this three-day flight to Lagos consisted of K-rations—hardly appetizing, but it was all we had.

Finally, we touched down in Lagos, Nigeria. I quickly went to the cable office to let Ned know where I was. Ned would send me a telegram back to tell me that he loved me and missed me so much.

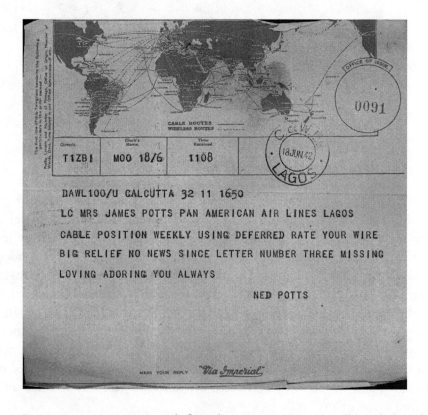

Once more, we met up with friends in Lagos. We were all headed in the same direction—to the United States—but it seemed that we were never on the same flight at the same time. So much depended on what time of day we would arrive at the flight office and how many people were in line ahead of us. Sometimes, people would be detained for no apparent reason, delaying their departures for days, even weeks.

While in Lagos, I was approached by a tall American who asked, "Aren't you Ginny Potts?" He told me his name was Harry Hawkins, and we had met in Calcutta where he had dated my best friend, Dot! Time and time again I was always amazed at what a small world we lived in.

Harry was staying in a chummery with some other men from Standard Oil, and he invited me to join him for dinner. I told him that I was not alone but traveling with a large group of friends, and he invited me to bring them all along.

After dinner that evening, we were all treated to a movie in one of the airplane hangars. The US military would fly in movies, and the hangars became makeshift movie theaters. There were no seats; we had to bring a blanket and sit on the ground. Troops and civilians mingled together and enjoyed the show. As I was sitting there, I was so surprised to see a young man I recognized sitting in front of me: George Thompson, a friend of my brother Jack. It seemed that no matter where I went around the world, there was a familiar face!

George and I chatted about home and what had brought each of us to Africa. He was working for Standard Oil and living near the Yabba guesthouse where I was staying while I waited several weeks for a flight out of Africa. I was happy to have George's company and the opportunity to escape the awful food at the guesthouse. I enjoyed many meals at his house, and I was intrigued by his two pet apes that had the run of the house.

During the day, the other women and I would spend time walking on the beach. It was so hot that catching a sea breeze was the best way to stay comfortable. Avocados were a staple in our diet. We would fill them with French dressing, grab a spoon, and sit on the beach enjoying the sea breeze and talking. One of the girls made herself a bikini from some local cotton material and was able to take advantage of the cool water. The other women were able to swap clothes. I wished that I too could swap clothes, but since I was so much taller, I was stuck wearing the same outfits over and over.

When I left India, I was only allowed to take a suitcase weighing thirty-five pounds. In those days, the suitcases alone weighed nearly that. They were made of sturdy leather and designed to withstand a gorilla stampede! I was only able to pack one pair of slacks, a skirt, two blouses, and a dress. I had also chosen to take the silver brush and mirror set Mother had given me for my sixteenth birthday. To heck with clothes—I wasn't about to leave one of my most treasured possessions behind.

After six weeks in Lagos, we were finally able to catch a bomber to Miami. The plane had no seats whatsoever. Marge, Fran, and I sat on the hard metal floor with only a thin blanket to cushion our bottoms. I was also lugging around a gift from George—a huge ebony carved bust of a Zulu warrior. It was a nuisance to carry, but I loved it and didn't want to leave it behind!

I didn't feel well during this flight. I had a fever and just assumed that all this travel and not enough rest or food was finally catching up with me. After a long plane trip that is only a blur in my memory, we finally landed in Miami, Florida. At last we had arrived safely on American soil!

CHAPTER TWENTY-ONE

Home Safe and Sound on American Soil

The first thing the customs officer did when we arrived in Miami was to confiscate our passports. We were told that during the war, we were forbidden to travel outside the United States, with the exception of Canada. I was relieved that I would still be able to visit my mother-in-law, Minn, in Ontario.

Marge, Fran, and I had arrived in Miami very late at night, long after the dining room at our hotel had closed. No matter—after fourteen weeks of what could best be described as "economy class" travel, tops on our agenda was a warm bath and a comfortable bed.

It was so wonderful to have real beds, a real shower, and yes, real towels! The towels in Africa, thin and sun-dried, felt like sandpaper. We felt like royalty in the hotel in Miami.

We were tired but not so tired that we couldn't call the front desk and arrange for a limousine the next day to take us on a shopping spree. All three of us had been wearing the same clothes for so long that we could hardly contain our excitement at the thought of buying new outfits.

The next morning, we savored our traditional American-style breakfast of eggs, bacon, toast, orange juice, and coffee before starting out on our shopping trip. Then it was off to Saks. We needed everything—bras, panties, girdles, stockings, slips, dresses, slacks, shoes, and hats. Our clothes were so worn and faded that we asked the saleslady to throw them away, and we wore our new purchases from dresses to undies out of the store. Next, it was on to the hair salon.

Fran and I had been able to book our appointments at the same time, but Marge's appointment was later, so we had all agreed to meet at the hotel restaurant afterwards. Imagine our surprise when Marge walked in, her hair soaking wet and tears running down her cheeks. "What happened?" We asked in unison.

"I have head lice," she managed to tell us in between sobs. Of course we knew they were highly contagious, so we made a quick trip to the drugstore to buy special shampoo. We spent the next hour or so treating her for lice. After everything we had been through over the past few months, this seemed like such a small problem—something we would be able to laugh about years later.

It was a bittersweet moment when the time came for the three of us to say our good-byes in Miami. Fran and I were continuing on to New York, but Marge was headed to Cleveland. How do you say good-bye to a friend with whom you have shared so much—the weeks of uncertainty as we waited to get out of India, the flights that were uncomfortable and frightening, the feelings we shared when we finally arrived safely in the United States, and that one glorious day in Miami? We hugged tightly and promised to stay in touch! We were not sure when we would see one another again.

When Fran and I arrived in New York, my family was there to greet us. Mother and Daddy had expected me to be a waif in well-worn clothes. Imagine their surprise when they saw this "fresh young thing" stepping off the train. I hadn't told them about our day of pampering in Miami.

Finally, it was off to Five Buttonwood Road on Staten Island. I had so much catching up to do with family and friends. I hadn't even met my brother Jack's wife, Polly. But before I could get too excited about everything I wanted to do in New York, my mysterious fever returned. Jack, who was interning at a hospital in New York City, stopped by for a visit. Like all doctors in those days, he had a little black bag, with everything one needed to make house calls. He took a blood sample and brought it back to the hospital lab to be analyzed. Apparently, I had contracted malaria, which can only be detected when the host is running a fever. So for the next several days, it was bed rest and quinine for me.

It was good to be safe in New York with my family, but my heart was heavy with longing and worry for Ned. In the nearly six years we had been together, we had never been separated for so long. I wished more than anything that I could be with him, but that just wasn't possible.

Despite everything he was going through, Ned never stopped being concerned about my happiness. He had written Father to ask him a favor:

5 Rainy Park
Calcutta
July 8th, 1942

Dear John:

Ginny and I have been married for nearly six years and it has been six years of heaven. In all that time, we have never had a fight—one or the other would always give in and it has been a perfect marriage. The coming months (I hope it is not years) with their loneliness and "blue days" will be grim and I want to do everything I possibly can to keep Ginny smiling.

Living twelve thousand miles and Lord knows how long in mail time away, it is difficult to do this unless I make some standing arrangements that will carry on regardless of whether or not we are cut off. It is for that reason that I am asking the favor.

Could you arrange with Hama or your secretary to send Ginny little gifts regularly ... It is hard to describe in detail what I mean by "little gifts" but I am thinking of ... a dozen roses, a bunch of violets, some gardenias, a box of chocolates or toffee (especially salt water toffee) or salted nuts or clear mints, one of those special gift baskets of fruit (especially apples), etc. And by regularly, I mean every ten days or two weeks ... the important thing is that Ginny receives something from her old man (as she calls me) regularly.

Then there are some extra special days when I would like Ginny to get both flowers and candy. They are:

Her birthday—July 31st

Our wedding anniversary—November 25th

The day we first met—October 13th

Also, Christmas, Valentine's Day and Easter

I know you will take good care of her but I can't help saying anyway "take good care of her." She is all I have and means everything to me. When the time came for her to go it was the hardest decision I ever had to make. I will keep my fingers crossed that this letter gets through to you and I will await your cable.

Much love,

Ned

Even from twelve thousand miles away, Ned managed to spoil me! I couldn't help wondering how different my life would have turned out if I had decided not to go on that blind date on October 13, 1936.

Ned waiting for Ginny to return

Hanging out with the guys

Where is my partner

Once I had recovered from malaria, my civic-minded father made sure I was kept busy. Father had served in the Judge Advocate General (JAG) Corps during World War I, and he wanted to do his part during this war too. He served on the mayor's committee, was in charge of the USO (United Service Organizations), and was an air warden—he was into everything!

Every Thursday evening, our family would go down to the USO on Staten Island and serve dinner to the troops. Mother worked for the Travelers Aid and helped families to find housing while they were serving their country.

Father was not shy about volunteering me for whatever needed to be done—I didn't really mind since I needed to keep busy.

Newspaper article Ginny out on the Town with Capt. Frank I. Higgs

A quick sketch done by Milton Caniff. The creator of "Terry and the Pirates"

I also made time to visit Ned's mother, Minn, in Canada and his uncle Burt Faulkner, who was minister of health in the Canadian government.

Ginny with Ned's mother, Minn

I stayed several weeks with Minn, who was not in the best of health. With her only child so far away, I did the best I could to care for her.

On one of my visits with Uncle Burt, I happened to answer a phone call at his house. It turned out to be a stroke of fate. It was the police who had word that Burt's son, Albert, had been killed in a car accident; and because of his government position, they did not want Burt to be notified until they could get medical help to his house in case he suffered a heart attack. The police asked me to screen all his calls until a doctor arrived.

Well, the doctor didn't arrive until after midnight, and I ended up intercepting many calls and telling the callers they had dialed the wrong number or else giving them the runaround. What a long, stressful night that was!

Shortly after Albert's funeral, I met with Peggy, who was married to Ned's best friend, Buster. Peggy arranged a meeting between me and her brother, David Mansur, who was a high-ranking official in the Canadian government.

David told me that travel restrictions were being lifted for Canadians and that he could get me a Canadian passport so that I could travel back to India to be reunited with Ned. I told him to make all the arrangements as soon as possible. I was ecstatic at the thought!

Back home in New York, I could hardly contain my excitement, and I started checking the mail every day for my passport. Well, it never arrived, but a letter from US government censors did. They informed me that my passport had been confiscated because passports could not be mailed between countries. If I wanted a Canadian passport, the letter said, I would have to return to Canada and apply for one.

I returned to Canada, thinking that it would be a simple process to obtain a Canadian passport—after all, I was married to a Canadian and thought I could hold dual citizenship.

Unfortunately, that was not the case. I was told if I wanted a Canadian passport, I would have to renounce my American citizenship. Renounce my American citizenship? I was very upset at the thought, even if it meant the chance to be reunited with Ned. I returned to my hotel to think seriously about what I should do. Frankly, I was feeling sorry for myself and spent half my time crying.

Finally, I pulled myself together enough to call my father for advice. I asked him if he thought I should renounce my citizenship or wait it out and hope the war would be over soon.

There was a long pause on the other end as my father, in typical fashion, carefully weighed his response. "What do you think Ned would say, after so many months of separation, if you were not willing to accept his nationality?"

I gulped and knew he was right. The next morning, I went back to the passport office and, with a heavy heart, signed away my American citizenship. I cried tears of joy and sorrow. I was so happy at the thought of being reunited with the man I loved yet sad beyond words to give up my citizenship, which was a huge decision. There was no turning back. I would not be an American again.

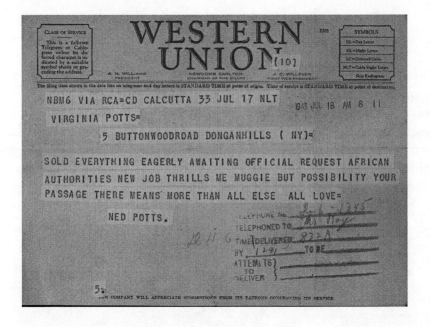

CHAPTER TWENTY-TWO

Ned's Arms Here I Come!

Before I could plan my trip back to India, Ned had been reassigned to South Africa, where he was helping the British army make supplies for the war effort. I was relieved that he was farther away from the fighting, but he wasn't any closer to me. He had to sell our furniture and pack up all of our belongings and ship them out of India by freighter, due to arrive in South Africa at the end of November.

He cabled me:

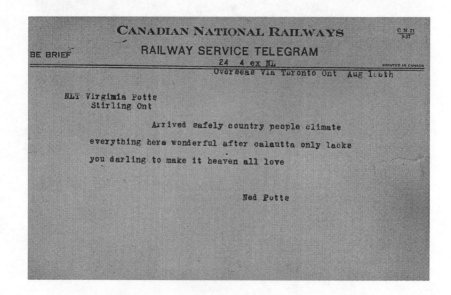

Ned had no idea before he left India that I would be joining him in South Africa. I cabled the news to him and told him that I planned to take a ship from Buenos Aires to Cape Town, South Africa. His biggest concern was my safety. We were in the midst of a world war after all, and international travel was considered very, very risky.

Well, there was no question after everything I'd been through. I had renounced my American citizenship after all; I was willing to take the risk to be with the man I loved! Mother and Father were very supportive of my plans to be reunited with Ned, which made things a little easier as I prepared to say good-bye.

Still, there was a lot of sadness the day they drove me to Penn Station. We all had heavy hearts, and this time we didn't even try to hold back our tears. So much was unknown—we didn't know what challenges I would face on my trip or when we would see each other again.

As the train picked up speed leaving Penn Station, I was overwhelmed with love and gratitude for my family. Through my tears, Mother and Father were a blur on the platform, and my throat ached from trying to hold back sobs. I had spent the last year in New York, longing to be with Ned, but at the same time, so fortunate to be living with my family.

As far as I was concerned, there would be one bright spot on my trip; from Philadelphia to Miami, I had been told my train would make a brief stop in Columbia, South Carolina, where my best friend, Dot, and her husband, Bill, were stationed. I had contacted Dot, and our plan was to meet at the train station, even if only for a few minutes. There was so much I wanted to tell her; I didn't even know where I would start! Imagine my disappointment when the train never even went anywhere near Columbia, South Carolina.

I arrived in Miami a day and a half after leaving New York and was greeted by one of my old high school friends, Lib Briggs, and her husband, Rex. We were all staying at the Miami Colonial Hotel and had planned to spend the next few days sightseeing before I was scheduled to take a plane out of Miami headed to Barranquilla in Colombia, South America. We did some sightseeing, but I also had to spend time taking care of business.

I can't wait to get to Ned.

Ginny and Lib

Ginny and Rex

It seemed that my travel papers and my immunizations weren't exactly in order, and I wouldn't be allowed to leave the country unless I straightened things out. I had to make several trips to the American consulate and also had to have more shots. Thank goodness Rex and Lib had a car and were able to chauffeur me around to tie up those loose ends.

On my last night in Miami, I wrote a long letter home, trying to express some of what I was feeling about leaving family behind after a wonderful year together:

> September 1943
> Dearest All:
>   Well tonight is my last night in the Good Old U.S.A. and it's hard to put into words how much I'm going to miss it all, especially you at home—you've been so perfect always but this year in particular has shown me more than ever how much I miss while I'm away. It won't ever be possible to thank you sufficiently for all the wonderful and generous things you've done but maybe someday I can express myself more articulately; right now about all I'm capable of is to say

"I love you" all with all my heart and thank you from the bottom of it many times over.

Lib and Rex were here at the hotel when I arrived and had a room under mine. I went to Pan American and found I needed a couple more visas and as Rex and Lib had their car they drove me around to consulates and doctors and such. I took Jack's advice about the aspirin and had no reactions whatsoever from my last two injections today. Tell him maybe he'll make a good doctor after all.

Discovered your check on the train, Mother, but tore it up so I wouldn't be tempted to spend it. You've been far, far, too generous to me as it is and I love you for every bit of it but I couldn't take it as I told you, so spend it for something you want instead. Thanks just the same, darling, but it's about time I get back into a harness for a change.

This last year has been such fun but it seems incredible that it has gone. We may not have done the things we planned but certainly had fun doing what we did.

Wish you could see all the palaver you have to go through down here—red tape is too mild a term. Tomorrow I go as far as Barranquilla and the next day on to Cali. From Cali on to Lima and there on to Santiago and finally Buenos Aires. I'll write and tell you all about things from Buenos Aires.

A million thanks to each of you and all of my love always.
Gia

CHAPTER TWENTY-THREE

South America: A Test of My Patience

The next day, I went to the airport at the crack of dawn to catch my first flight out of Miami headed to Barranquilla, Colombia. Things didn't go well. The first customs officer I encountered was nasty and wouldn't allow me on the plane because I didn't have a note from the American consul stating when and where I had renounced my citizenship.

Apparently the information from Canada had not been properly forwarded to authorities in the United States. I didn't know what to do. I wandered about the airport on the verge of tears, thinking about how to handle my first major hurdle.

Finally, the customs official agreed to call someone in authority, who quizzed me at length over the phone. That person agreed to let me pass, but from there I had to make it through Customs, Immigration, the Navy Department, Department of Internal Revenue, and the censors. By this time, I was practically "sweating blood" for fear they might change their minds at the last minute. When I received the final okay, I burst through the doors to board the plane in record time.

My traveling companions on the flight were an interesting mix of people. There was a Mr. Huggins with his wife and three daughters, on their way to Jamaica where he was about to take the position as governor general. They seemed a bit pompous to me, but we struck up a conversation, and I discovered I didn't have to curtsey after all. There was also a blonde woman going to Colombia to marry a man she had not seen in two years—she was sick during the entire flight; a seismograph expert and his wife were headed to a remote jungle area for two years—his wife said she would be crying the whole time. Then there was the Scotsman with the wooden leg, his wife, and two-year-old son. They caused quite a commotion when the mother tripped and fell while carrying the toddler to the lavatory, and his head split open.

The pilot had to radio ahead to Cienfuegos, Cuba, and request permission to land, which we received. We all waited on the plane while the family went to the hospital for the baby to get stitches.

Our next stop was in Jamaica. Here all the passengers were treated to Planters Punches, courtesy of one of the large rum companies. By the time we reboarded the plane for Barranquilla, many of the passengers were "tighter than ticks."

I wasn't in that state, but wouldn't you know that our pilot for the next leg of the journey was a member of the Short Snorters Club? He invited me into the cockpit, and I had a few drinks. By the time we landed in Barranquilla, I was feeling a little tipsy too.

We were taken to the Prado Hotel, a very fashionable place with lighted terraces around the swimming pool and an outdoor dance floor. Because the hotel was so full, I ended up sharing a room with another American woman who was going to live and work in the jungle. As she described her housing—a hut built on stilts to keep out snakes and bugs—I found myself thinking that my early life in India hadn't been so bad after all.

At six the next morning, we took a bus to the airport and faced more red tape and delays before we were finally allowed to board a short flight to Medellin, Colombia. There were many passengers in Medellin preparing to travel to Cali, Columbia, my next destination. During the flight, I chatted with Mr. Vincent, a very nice Columbian gentleman who was in the textile business. Apparently he was engaged to an American woman whose father was the president of General Electric. Mr. Vincent was kind enough to offer me a ride from the airport to the Hotel Columbus where we were both staying. Since I spoke no Spanish at all, I was grateful for the offer. When we checked into adjacent rooms with a shared balcony, however, I started to feel a little uncomfortable. I wasn't sure what Mr. Vincent's intentions were toward me, so that night I locked my doors and pulled my drapes. The next morning, I told the hotel desk clerk that the light from the balcony was shining in my eyes and asked for a room change.

Mr. Vincent invited me to join him at his country club the next day, saying I could swim and relax by the pool while he played golf. Still feeling uncomfortable around him, I politely declined the invitation. I told him I had to catch up on my letter writing.

I did meet some other interesting people while staying at the Hotel Columbus. One chap from Texas was with the Federal Bureau of Investigation we spent a few afternoons at the country club together. Another gentleman who was at my table each night for dinner was from Canada. He was working for the Canadian Machine Company and knew all about Stirling, Ned's hometown. He also spoke Spanish, which was a big plus in my estimation.

A man who was in the coffee business invited me to a dance. It turned out that he was familiar with Dongan Hills, my neighborhood on Staten Island. Here I was at a small hotel in South America, and I had already met two people—one who knew about Ned's small town in Ontario and the other who was familiar with my neighborhood. It was just amazing to me to continually run into people who knew somebody or someplace that was near and dear to my heart.

I was up at the crack of dawn again, this time scheduled to take a flight to Lima, Peru. But I was told my seat had been given to a priority passenger, and I would have to wait. To say I was fuming was an understatement. My frustration only grew as my wait turned from hours into days. Each day I would appear at the airport and try to plead my case, but to no avail—this was wartime. I was told repeatedly I would just have to wait.

One afternoon, I was sitting in my hotel room feeling sorry for myself when the phone rang. It was an American by the name of Duke Surre; he was staying at the hotel and had noticed that I was alone. He invited me to join him for drinks and dinner. I agreed to meet him at 6:00 p.m., and within thirty minutes, we were playing the "do you know?" game. He too knew Dongan Hills and even knew some of the same people I did. It turned out Duke was an airport engineer with Pan American Airlines. After I told him my sob story about being unable to get a flight out of Cali, he offered to pull some strings and get me a flight the next day. He called the airline and told them I was the wife of an old college friend; and wouldn't you know, he arranged for me to fly to Lima, Peru, the next morning. I was ecstatic.

After dinner, Duke escorted me back to my room, and his body language suggested he was waiting for an invitation to come inside. I told him I was happily married and quickly closed the door. I thought sure that refusing his advance would doom my chances of getting on the flight the next day. But it turned out that Duke was a man of his word. I was on a flight to Lima the next morning.

One of the first things I did when I arrived in Lima was to try to book a flight to Santiago, Argentina. I was told that it would be a week to ten days before that might happen. I was getting so tired of all the delays, the uncertainty, and the waiting. Not being able to speak Spanish just added to my frustration—I went back to my hotel and had a good cry.

The next morning, I sent cables to Ned and my mother and father, letting them know I was safe but still trying to make my way to South Africa. Later I was sitting in my room reading when the phone rang. It was Duke Surre and his wife calling from the hotel lobby—they invited me to join them for a drink. He has a wife! What a relief. I started to think maybe I had imagined his advances at the hotel in Cali. But none of that mattered now—he had kept his word and was able to get me on a flight to Lima. When I met Duke and his wife, I explained my current dilemma, and once again, Duke offered to help. He arranged my flight and even gave me a letter of introduction to officials in Santiago, my next stop. Now I felt like I could relax a bit. The next day, I hired an English-speaking cabdriver and set out to see some of the sights in Lima with a new friend in tow—a young American woman who spoke Spanish very well. We not only enjoyed the sights, we painted the town red.

When I arrived at the airport the next morning, I was surprised to receive a beautiful corsage of three white orchids, a gift from Duke. With my purple dress and lovely white orchids, I felt like Mrs. Astor—a famous New York socialite of the time.

The flight from Lima to Santiago was twelve hours long and included many stops to refuel and get a bite to eat. I was so happy once we landed to be greeted at my hotel by my friends, Fran and Bill. They were living in Santiago, and Fran was due to have a baby any day. At dinner that evening, I took advantage of the fact that Santiago is known for its beef and ordered a large steak. It was so tender and delicious; I wished I could pack some to take with me.

The next morning, I was back at the airport for my scheduled flight to Buenos Aires, Argentina, only to find out it had been cancelled. I learned that unless I wanted to stay in Santiago for another two weeks, my only option was to take a small plane across the Andes Mountains to Mendoza, Argentina, and then from there, take the train to Buenos Aires, Argentina.

Sixteen people, myself included, decided to take the flight. And what a breathtaking one it was! As we took off at sunrise the next day, the sunlight and the cloud formations over the snow-covered Andes were spectacular. How I wish I could have taken pictures, but it was forbidden due to wartime security. You were not allowed to travel with a camera.

When we arrived in Mendoza, we had to go through customs, but this was customs like I had never experienced it before. They checked us very thoroughly—so thoroughly that we all missed our train to Buenos Aires. So it was back to a hotel for one more night and then off to the station in the morning to catch the train.

CHAPTER TWENTY-FOUR

Traveling with Helena Rubinstein

I was surprised to hear banging on my door early the next morning. The woman in the room next to mine wanted to be sure I would make the train. We had been "smiling friends" since leaving Lima but hadn't really spoken. All the while I had been intrigued by this very short woman, compared to myself. You couldn't help but notice her: She was decked out in jewels—diamond earrings the size of my thumbnail, a jade bracelet with pearls the size of crab apples, and a choker necklace with huge beads carved from emeralds. She also wore ruby rings the size of plums on both hands. Her hair was long, black, and pulled into a bun. Compared to my lack of makeup, hers seemed rather extreme. She wore a lot of makeup: Her bright pink rouge looked like it had been applied with a donut. To top it off, she was wearing vibrant-colored clothes from the latest Paris designers. She may have been short but she was a stunning woman. It was hard not to miss her.

Helena Rubinstein

It wasn't until we shared a cab to the train station that I learned that this intriguing woman was Princess Helena Gourielli, better known as Helena Rubinstein—the founder and head of a cosmetic empire and one of the wealthiest women in the world.

I was never really sure why, but Helena took me under her wing. During our long train ride, we shared meals and stories and even played bridge. It was wonderful to have her companionship. She was a very interesting woman and made me feel safer to know I was in the company of such a world traveler—a woman of the world with charm, confidence, and compassion.

When we arrived in Buenos Aires at midnight, there was no one from Union Carbide to greet me. It was customary for a young lady to have an escort; apparently the cable I'd sent had never arrived. There was, however, a small horde of photographers to greet Helena. It was midnight in Buenos Aires, but the press was there following her every move. Flashbulbs blinded us as we departed the train. Helena was kind and invited me to stand with her for a few photos, but I politely declined. I figured no one would know who I was—a giant young woman standing next to a gorgeous, world-renowned businesswoman. Looking back now, I wish I had agreed to have my picture taken with her. What a wonderful souvenir it would have made.

When Helena realized that I was alone to make my way to my hotel, she decided it wasn't proper for a young lady to be out alone at this time of night. She insisted that I stay with her at her apartment. She had an entourage of people attending to her every need. Once her huge pile of luggage had been loaded into a big black limousine, we were off for a ride to an apartment in the city, where she was staying while her house was being renovated. She apologized profusely about how small the apartment was, but she should have saved her apologies: The place was luxurious by my standards. I had a bath drawn and waiting for me, and my every wish was quickly taken care of.

It was fun and exciting to spend time with one of the wealthiest and most fascinating women in the world. She showed me photos of some of the other houses she owned—one in Paris and another in New York—and her beautiful furnishings, many of them treasured antiques. I started daydreaming about what it must be like to have that kind of wealth and to be able to decorate anyway you'd like. But I quickly came to my senses and realized that I was lucky in my own way.

Helena was in Buenos Aires for the grand opening of a new salon and corporate offices in South America. She already had corporate offices in Paris, London, New York, and who knows where else. She was far ahead of her time—a woman of great power at a time when most women had very little, if any power, in the corporate world.

She invited me to visit her salon before the grand opening. It was as exquisitely decorated as her home. She also took me along on a few shopping excursions to find just the right finishing touches—no expense was being spared. Helena's vision was to have flowers cascading down the facade of the salon like a colorful waterfall. She spent hours trying to find just the right furnishings and other items to add to the salon's décor. She knew the women of Buenos Aires would welcome a lavish salon that catered to their exclusive tastes. The atmosphere here felt a lot like Fifth Avenue in New York to me.

A woman of the world but she had a heart of gold.
I was so fortunate to have crossed paths with her.

Sadly, the day arrived when I had to leave Helena's apartment and go to the Plaza Hotel. It was nice enough, but I missed the lavish treatment I had received at Helena's. I quickly became busy, connecting with old friends and making new ones. I called Helen and Leon Brittan, a couple I knew from India, now stationed in Buenos Aires. They invited me to their house for dinner, where I met Charlie Sheehan, a man who worked for National City Bank in Connecticut. Charlie knew Ned's boss, Mr. MacKenzie, who in fact, had asked him to look me up while he was in Buenos Aires. It turned out that Charlie was scheduled to go to South Africa on the same ship I was and was staying at my hotel.

During my six-week scheduled "layover" in Buenos Aires, Charlie, who was much older, became a father figure to me. He would take me out to dinner whenever I didn't have plans and was always looking out for my welfare. I also spent time with the Lechners, a Union Carbide couple who took me to see all kinds of sights and kept me busy. The city had a very strong European influence rather than the typical Spanish style, and the architecture reflected that. The Teatro Colon was one of the world's great opera houses. Jardin Botanico, the botanical garden, was especially beautiful. There were three gardens dedicated to one special style, Roman, Greek, and Oriental, each with trees from the country of origin. Statues and works of art were also placed throughout the grounds. The zoo was also a great place to while away the hours till I sailed. And last, but not least, The Obelisk, a tall pillar rising 229 feet in the air in a square where locals held rallies and laborers gathered to demonstrate. In all, I learned a lot about the city and its culture. Did you know that the tango, originated in Buenos Aires and the name Buenos Aries means "fair winds." The people are called Portenos, which means "people of the port"?

CHAPTER TWENTY-FIVE

Sailing to South Africa at Last

Just as our departure date arrived, we learned that the ship to South Africa had been cancelled because the Germans had sunk a number of ships, and it was considered too risky to set out to sea. I was heartbroken. I had traveled for so long and so far and was now being told it might be a month or so before another ship would sail out. Ned too was devastated by the news that our much-anticipated reunion had been delayed again.

Charlie was not so quick to give up. He busied himself working on an alternate plan and contacted a sea captain whose ship had been used for the black market trade to South Africa. The captain had two cabins left and was willing to take three passengers—Charlie and another man would share a cabin, and I would have the other cabin to myself. Charlie was not sure if I would want to take a chance on a cargo ship. He did not, however, know my determination to reach Ned. Was I willing to go? Without a moment's hesitation, I said yes! The only thing in our way that could put an end to our passage was a torpedo, and that was a reality I did not wish to dwell on. Charlie informed me that living conditions would be hard, and we would have to bring our own drinking water, cigarettes, liquor, cards, books, and any other things we needed to keep us occupied for about seventeen days. It was just like traveling the back roads of India, so I was well prepared.

Once I saw the *Ambu*, I had second thoughts. The ship was far worse than anything I had sailed on before. Built before World War I, it was an iron freighter with a very rusty hull. I later learned that it had been sunk by the Germans during the First World War, and a salvage company had refloated it and sold it to an Argentinean company for the black market trade.

The Lechners, who had graciously taken me to the pier to see me off, were in shock. "Oh my," was Mr. Lechner's polite reaction. He told me he didn't think it was a wise idea to "take this tub to Africa."

"I don't think it will make it past the breakwater." His voice was just a whisper.

There I stood on the pier, just an hour before the wretched-looking *Ambu* was set to sail. It was the end of October, and all I could think about was how much I wanted to be with Ned for our anniversary in November. I guess my judgment was clouded with the thought of holding Ned in my arms and giving him a big kiss.

Nothing was going to deter me. I boarded the ship, along with Charlie Sheehan and the third passenger, an Englishman named Mr. Drake, a rather unpleasant young man who seemed to have nothing but sexual exploits on his mind. I certainly didn't think I was boarding a luxury cruise liner—but I also didn't realize that this decrepit ship was built strictly for cargo, not passengers. That reality had not sunk in when Charlie first told me about the ship; however, it was very apparent now. My head grazed the ceiling of my tiny cabin, and my outstretched arms nearly reached both walls. There was no running water in my cabin and only one bathroom on the whole ship—which was out of order most of the time. Getting to it was the worst part of the ordeal, down the hall and through the mess hall, which always had a few crew members, and the stares and whispers were very disconcerting. What was worse for me was the stench of garlic on the mattress in my tiny cabin. No matter what I did, it wouldn't go away. The guy who had slept there before must have drooled on the mattress. I shuddered at the thought, sprinkled perfume on the mattress, and tried to picture the Ritz.

I was the only female with a crew of fifty men and my two male traveling companions. Most of the crew spoke only Spanish, so there was little conversation. Each morning, Charlie would knock on my cabin door to let me know the bathroom was free, and I would make my way through the dining room in my flower-print bathrobe and white mules. At first, the crew members would whisper and point, but by the end of the trip, they had grown accustomed to seeing me on my morning trek to the bathroom.

Life aboard ship was no fun, and the days stretched on endlessly. There were no deck chairs—there wasn't even a deck to speak of. All we could do was sit on the hatches and take three steps in one direction for exercise. The deck was also where the cook stored the meat—or I should say livestock. There was a small pen of chickens and goats that would be slaughtered one by one for our evening meals. Our vegetables were stored in a lifeboat, and each day the cook would sort through them: the rotten ones would be tossed overboard, the ones on the verge of rotting were served at dinner, and the freshest ones were kept for the next day. Of course, they would be on the verge of rotting.

Fortunately, Charlie and I were compatible, and we shared some nice conversations during this otherwise miserable voyage. At night we would go topside and enjoy a drink of scotch while gazing at the stars, which were so bright against the dark sky. Charlie pointed out the Southern Cross which can only be seen if you are in the southern hemisphere. "The sky is filled with stars you can only view if you are south of the equator," he would say.

Despite the condition of the *Ambu*, it was fairly smooth sailing for our seventeen days at sea, even if it felt more like three months. I wasn't aware that any enemy ship had been spotted and never felt threatened, but we did not speak Spanish, so we would not have had any inkling of danger.

I had cabled ahead to let Ned know my estimated date of arrival. For security reasons, I wasn't allowed to divulge information about what we were arriving on or our exact arrival, just in case the cable was seized by enemy hands. There was a saying back then "loose lips sink ships," so all was very hush-hush. I used code times and dates, referencing Jack's birthday and his graduation less mother's name numerically. I think you get an idea of the situation. Ned was determined to be at the pier to meet me when we docked. Ned took a colleague named John Berwick along for company and safety. They set out by car from Port Elizabeth to Cape Town seven days before my expected arrival.

November 17, 1943:

Ned had been waiting dockside for five days when the *Ambu* finally arrived in port. The ship was so small that he couldn't even see it above the dock line. Finally, realizing we were in port, Ned tried to rush out to greet me; but of course, we had to wait for customs to come aboard and for the cargo to be unloaded before we could disembark. All Ned and I could do was smile and wave at each other for what seemed like an eternity.

Finally, after more than a year and a half apart, followed by months of travel delays and frustrations—Ned and I were reunited in Cape Town, South Africa. Even though I had been cramped on a tiny ship with hardly any running water for nearly three weeks, I had carefully chosen the outfit I would wear when Ned first set eyes on me: It was a rose gabardine suit with a blouse that had a bow tied at the neck, a small black hat with a feather flower, alligator shoes, and a matching bag completed the look. "Wow! You look like a million bucks," Ned whispered, as he took me into his arms.

Cape Town, South Africa:

How can I describe what it felt like to finally be back together with Ned? Those first few hours, I was so giddy with happiness. It almost felt like a dream. To add to it all, Ned had planned our reunion down to the last detail. He whisked me away to a hotel on the outskirts of town, overlooking the ocean. When I set foot in our room, I could hardly believe my eyes: it was filled with flowers of all kinds, dozens of carnations, talisman roses, red roses, and orchids. There was a new suit for me to wear, a box of chocolates, and music playing from a portable radio Ned had brought with him.

If I had ever questioned the heartache and frustration I endured to be reunited with Ned during the war, I knew in an instant in that hotel room that I had done the right thing: Ned was the most kind, loving, and romantic husband a woman could ever ask for.

We held each other close I wanted to never let him go. We spent hours talking about everything that had happened in our lives while we were apart. He told me all about the house he had waiting for me in Port Elizabeth. Ned and I talked for hours. That night, we went out on the town and let our hair down, something we hadn't been able to do for almost two years. The war seemed far, far away. We were deeply in love, and this was *our* time at last.

We took a cable car to the top of Table Mountain, one of the most gorgeous spots in all of South Africa. From high atop this plateau, we could see Cape Town's lights for miles, as well as the stars and the ocean. I had crossed continents and oceans to be with Ned, and here we were finally in each other's arms again, ready to begin the next chapter of our lives together.

I still marvel to think about the carefree young woman living a comfortable life on Staten Island in 1936. I had no clue when I decided to go on a blind date on October 13 that my whole life was about to change beyond my wildest imaginings. And it all happened because I met a young man, Ned Potts, who swept me off my feet. I wasn't sure about too much back then, but I was confident enough to follow my heart and to accept Ned's impetuous marriage proposal. By the time we were reunited in Cape Town, South Africa, after being separated by World War II, I was certain of at least one thing: from the start, Ned and I were destined to share a life filled with love and adventure.

EPILOGUE

There is one sad note to this chapter of my parents' life that began in South Africa. The day before their seventh anniversary, they received a cable with the terrible news that the freighter carrying all their household and personal belongings from India had been sunk by the Japanese. Gone were their silver and china, my father's beloved cornet, my mother's sewing machine, and all their clothes. My father lost every bit of personal memorabilia he owned, including his yearbook, his school cups, and the only photo he had of his father.

It was next to impossible to replace many of their household furnishings while they were in South Africa due to wartime rationing. But my parents had faced challenges before, and they would face this one with their usual optimism and strength. What was most important was that they still had each other.

Eventually, they would share their love with a baby daughter they adopted from a hospital in Port Elizabeth. They named me Carolyn, which was shortened to Cali by a young friend of the family.

Mom and Dad and I left South Africa in 1947 and went back to India until 1954. Then Dad was transferred to the United States, where we settled in Greenwich, Connecticut. Dad rose through the ranks of Union Carbide Company, becoming vice chairman of the company before he retired.

Ned and Ginny spent their retirement years in Mexico, where my father died in 1992. They had spent fifty-six wonderful years of marriage.

There is one more happy note to Ginny's story. My mother was able to regain her American citizenship, thanks to a legislation proposed by her father, New York Congressman John H. Ray. The new law allowed wartime wives, who had given up their American citizenship to be with their husbands, to become citizens once again.

Additional Photographs of Interest

Little beggar boy with his pet monkey

Rickshaw stand in one of the villages in south India

A crowd would gather whenever Ned would stop to sell to dealers. We were certainly the attraction of the day.

Trichinopoly Cathedral—home to the Roman Catholic bishop

One of the many temples we saw on our visit to Madura. The symbol painted above the entrance is the symbol of man. The outline in white is man, and the red line inside is the menstrual flow symbolizing woman. Pilgrims worshiping in that temple have the same symbol painted on their foreheads.

Temple elephant, notice the same symbol painted on its forehead

Women looking at water pots in a shop in the bazaar in Trichinopoly

Barbershop set up on the sidewalk in Calcutta

A street entertainer in a red-and-blue-colored horse costume. However, the interesting thing about the photo is the polka dots on the wall. They are cow patties drying in the sun.

Very unusual dugout boats. These were from a particular tree that had exposed
roots from which the boats were made.

Spit Here, a sign often seen on the streets of major cities because the spit from
one's mouth is bright red and stains everything it touches. Betel nut is a leaf
pouch sold all over India at little stands. The betel leaf and the seed from the
areca palm are made into a little wrapped pouch called *paan*, which is chewed as
a breath freshener by a lot of Indians, mostly Hindus.

Coconut shells being loaded into boats to be sold to places that make coco fiber, which in turn is made into many products. A big business in India.

A native tapping a palm tree for, sap which is then fermented and turned into a very sweet potent drink. Said to have quite a kick, I was told.

Sugarcane being sold on the street, which is chewed like candy

A barber in the streets of Madras. Just sit yourself down, and they will come.

Ned and Ginny on tour. Wearing garlands which are a traditional part
of many Indian celebrations, sometimes made from flowers
and sometimes from gold and precious gems.

Ginny looking fetching

Ned and Ginny standing on the tennis court at Five Rainy Park, Calcutta.

Snake charmer

Ginny and Ruth Todd "home shopping." The tradesmen would bring their wares right to the house for us to peruse. We are looking over a selection of boxes from Kashmir, high-quality, hand-painted papier-mâché.

Marge Shafer relaxing in the yard in Calcutta

From the Land of "Terry and the Pirates" Is "Grett Murmur," --- City's Margaret Shafer

By ROY DE CRANE

THE Cleveland girl who is the "Grett Murmur" of Terry and the Pirates, Press comic strip, was back home today, bringing a story of the Asiatic war as thrilling as the comic strip itself.

In real life she is Mrs. Margaret Shafer, a 27-year-old brunette, who spent two years at the ends of the Himalaya "hump," the hottest air run in the world.

Mrs. Shafer is with her parents, Mr. and Mrs. Charles B. Ryan of 3833 E. 116th street, taking a quiet rest after adventures in India and China that led artist Milton Caniff to put her in his exciting picture-story.

Her adventures started in Calcutta, when she was there with her husband, Jacob K. Shafer, a National Carbon Co. representative, in 1940. Since then she has been known as a hostess for Americans, flyers at a terminus of the Himalaya route.

"Time was heavy on my hands," Mrs. Shafer said today. "With plenty of servants and little housework to do, I talked myself into a job."

Her job was teaching natives to bake apple pies and angel food cakes, and other American dishes, at a Calcutta ice cream store.

"The American population of 300 flocked to the place. When the China National Aviation Co. opened a Calcutta base in 1941, officials engaged Mrs. Shafer as their head chef, feeding American flyers hired by the Chinese.

The war moved closer, and Mrs. Shafer, with other American women, was evacuated back to the States. But the Chinese firm was still impressed. They found her here, engaged her to operate the hostel at the big Chinese base, feeding and entertaining Americans after their trip through Jap fire over the mountains.

Meanwhile, a Terry character in India had asked her to give his greetings to Artist Caniff in New York. Mr. Caniff asked Mrs. Shafer's permission to portray her in his feature.

"But I didn't really crash in the Himalayas as Grett Murmur, did," the brunette heroine said.

Mrs. Shafer was the only American woman at the unnamed base. The commercial and Army flyers coming there made the man-woman ratio 1000-to-1.

"At the dances, we never took more than three steps until another American pilot cut in," Mrs. Shafer said.

Mrs. Shafer ... "Grett Murmur" is back from India.

Article about Marge

Ginny atop a *ghari*

Moving Indian-style.

Holy man

A young girl bathing at a pump on the street

Water buffalo pulling a plow through a paddy field

A very young boy working on a brass lid with very crude tools, his hammer, a piece of wood, and bricks used as a vice to hold the lid in place.
His pay, a few annas a day.

Ginny at her ninety-first birthday, just before her death in 2004

GLOSSARY

anna:	Sixteen *annas* make a *rupee*, similar to our penny.
bearer:	Man servant head of the household help.
burra:	Big, important; *burra sahib* means "important man."
chit:	Note.
chokra:	Young assistant to the bearer.
chummery:	Shared household, usually of bachelors.
coolie:	Native porter; man or woman who do manual labor.
dak:	Post; *dak wallah*, postman; *dak* bungalow is a government-maintained house for the use of travelers and postman in rural India.
derzi:	Tailor or dress maker.
dhobi:	Laundry man who does the washing.
flat:	Apartment
ghari:	Horse-drawn cart.
ghats:	Steps along the river's edge leading down to the water.
gopuras:	Towers at Hindu temples.
gymkhana:	Sports club where sporting events are held, where both Indian and Europeans can be members.
Hindustani:	A simple form of Urdu, a language common in India.
khana:	Dinner.
maidan:	Public land, parade ground.
maharajah:	A ruler or lord of a state in India.
maharani:	Wife of a *maharajah*.
mali:	Gardener.
memsahib:	Madam or lady.
pi **dog**:	Mongrel dogs found all over India.
punkah:	Ceiling fan.

purdah: Seclusion, expected of high-class Indian women and some religious groups.

roti: Bread.

rupee: Indian currency.

sahib: Sir.

shamiana: A marquee, tent, spectator area.

tamasha: A word used in India by Europeans to describe a big party or gathering.

tank: Man-made lake, often a place of holy water.

tiffin: Lunch.

tonga: Two-wheeled, horse-drawn cart. The seats face out the back.

topee: Hat; pith helmet.

wallah: Man, *punkah wallah.*

Get Published, Inc!
Thorofare, NJ 08086
08 September 2009
BA2009251